# EVERY GOOD-BYE AIN'T GONE

*I hope I have shed light on the complexity of a people central to the American experience*

*[signature]*

*2/27/9*

# EVERY
# GOOD-BYE
# AIN'T GONE

*Family portraits*
*and*
*personal escapades*

## Itabari Njeri

Portions of this work originally appeared in *The Miami Herald*.

Permission acknowledgments for previously published material appear on page 246.

Library of Congress Cataloging-in-Publication Data
Njeri, Itabari.
    Every good-bye ain't gone / by Itabari Njeri.
        p.   cm.
    ISBN 0-8129-1805-3
    1. Njeri family.   2. Njeri, Itabari—Family.   3. Afro-Americans—Biography.   4. Afro-Americans—Social life and customs.   I. Title.
E185.96.N54   1990
973'.0496073022—dc20
    [B]                                                    89-40192

Manufactured in the United States of America

9 8 7 6 5 4 3 2

First Edition

Book design & decorative art by J. Vandeventer

For
my mother, my grandmother, my father and
Kay-Kay

*Every shut eye ain't sleep;*
*every good-bye ain't gone.*

—African-American proverb

# Contents

# Prelude

I remember a hat, a fast hat on crutches. Its wide, beige straw brim cut a bobbing but determined profile as the woman who wore it flung herself toward God. She was trim, she was suited, she had a broken leg in a cast. Two children were at her left and a coconspirator was at her right as she hopped on padded staffs to the Church of the Annunciation. There, God would redeem her and wash her children's sins away.

It was a day for miracles, Easter Sunday, and after almost fifteen years of marriage my mother had determined it was not too late to defy my father's atheism, his armchair Marxism, and reclaim her Catholic faith. And to get to the emotional nitty-gritty, it wasn't a bad way to get back at the brute for running her out of the house, then chasing her down several flights of stairs where she stumbled, fell and broke her leg—all because she had cleaned out his closet and thrown away some Harvard mementos.

I suspect that particular bit of housekeeping was an act of retribution in itself. My father's books, degrees and academic memorabilia were the tangible evidence of his awesome intellect and accomplishments, all of which he lorded over my mother, who was bright and beautiful but no intellectual. To her, clutter—no matter what its historical significance—needed to go. And though she loved a good book, why turn the house into a library when the public had already paid for one?

Mad and hatted, my mother was the image of deliberate locomotion, choosing a route that took her along the east side of Convent Avenue where City College stood. It was the same five blocks to the church from our Harlem apartment whichever side of the street she took, but to the east the blocks were longer, with fewer curbs she had to hop across. She and her longtime friend Mariella moved with a silent urgency neither my brother nor I understood.

Inside the beautiful gray stone church, the four of us stood at the baptismal font. The priest looked at my brother and me, then turned to my mother.

"How old are these children?" he asked.

She told him.

"I can baptize your son," the priest told her. "Your daughter is too old to be baptized without religious instruction." I was past seven, beyond the age of reason.

The priest looked sternly at my mother. It had been a long time since he'd run into so lapsed a Catholic. But she forged on; one out of two would have to do. And she told the priest that I would immediately be enrolled in catechism classes so that I could be baptized, too.

But it was too late. I was eleven and, intellectually, too much my father's child. To this day, I remain what my devoutly Catholic great-aunt May called "a heathen," believing I came into the world without sin and content to do the best I can while in it. My mother had early warnings I'd end up this way.

"Why do those children look like that?" I asked her, as we walked through our old Brooklyn neighborhood one afternoon. She was dressed in her navy blue, military-style visiting nurse's uniform, a jauntily placed field cap on her head. I often accompanied her on her rounds when I was four or five. I was about that age when we passed a park and saw the knot of children—bent, big-headed, twisted, pushed around on wheels. "Why?" I asked her, if God was so powerful, so merciful.

My mother answered honestly: "I don't know."

That was the first strike against God, which began my vague but persistent doubts of his existence. The childhood skepticism grew as I wondered how a kind and merciful God could let me witness my mother humiliated and in despair—over a hat.

It was a *baaaaddddd* hat. We'd been window-shopping on Fifth Avenue when my mother saw it. It was furlike and emerald green with a paisley scarf (studded with semiprecious stones) wrapped around the base of the crown. My mother took it off the mannequin's head and put it on her own. "Oooooh," she cooed at her mirrored image. But she took it off, put it back on the dummy's head and then we took the A train home in silence.

We got off the train at the 125th Street station and climbed the steep hill along St. Nicholas Terrace to our apartment. Just a few blocks from home my mother stopped. She rushed into a phone booth. She called my grandmother Ruby. She told her about the hat. "And it's green, Mama." My mother loved green. "It has these beautiful stones . . . and a scarf. . . ." And I heard my mother's voice quiver: "If you could just lend me . . . because . . . Please, Mama. . . . He won't even give me money for Kotex. . . ."

I was barely nine, my brother two, and my mother was only working sporadically as a nurse since his birth. I learned then, like many a daughter, what it meant for a woman to be without money of her own . . . feel trapped . . . be battered . . . need a hat.

More than twenty years have passed since my mother got that hat. When I last saw it, it was on my grandmother's head looking almost as fresh as the first day my mother wore it. And when she wore it, crowds parted, pulses quickened.

One Sunday, we took the A train south, back to Brooklyn, where my life began, back to our old brownstone apartment building in a neighborhood of Caribbean immigrants and African-American migrants from the South. With my brother and me at her side, she stepped from the foyer of a nineteenth-century row house onto its gray-white stone stoop. In high black pumps that accentuated the calves of her beautiful legs, she descended the steps as Josephine Baker would have, her emerald hat crowning her head.

An old, dark man slowed his languorous pace to watch her from the opposite side of the street. He wore a black wool coat, a red cravat, a black fedora. "Lovvvvely," he called out to her, lingering on the spoken caress, tipping his hat with one gloved hand, the other hand resting on his cane. Then he walked on more briskly. . . .

What follows on these pages began as a novel and ends up the literal truth; many might not have believed the portrayals otherwise.

Someone might have thought I pulled an archetype from a sociological tract to depict my father, the Afro-American intellectual in crisis.

Someone might have thought I was hallucinating when I put to paper a fraction of the life of my moll aunt—especially the day she stepped off a plane draped in white ermine and with hair dyed green for St. Patrick's Day framing her alabaster face.

Someone might have thought I was writing fiction with my eyes on a made-for-TV movie deal when I wrote that I searched through small southern towns to track down my grandfather's killer.

Someone might have thought I'd created a fictional character

# *Prelude*

who rejected her blackness had she been based on what I am: African, East Indian, Amer-Indian, English and French—common ancestral suspects for a member of the African diaspora. And yet, if I wrote as fiction that I am the great-great-great-granddaughter of a notorious, rum-running English pirate named Sam Lord—his castle now a resort in Barbados—someone would have said I was penning an improbable background for an African-American.

All these someones would have equaled most of America, because nobody really knows us. So institutionalized is the ignorance of our history, our culture, our everyday existence that, often, we do not even know ourselves.

Several names and a few details in this book have been changed to protect the privacy of family members and friends. But the characters in my family only seem made up. At times both comical and tragic, they *have* been too large for life.

Yet, if it's true that we choose our parents, choose the lives we come into, do not think me a masochist. Few writers have been offered a better bunch from which to spring. Few hearts have been nurtured in so bittersweet a nest. Because of my family, I learned early to see and hear the complexity and grand drama that underlay the simplest of human actions.

At times, when my family's grand dreams have seemed overly tragic, I remember that a discouraged soul is of use to no one; for I was taught, too, to persevere with grace. And then I imagine myself running past a crowd of mourners: I am waving, I am smiling, I am naked and have lost everything—but I am in a hat . . .

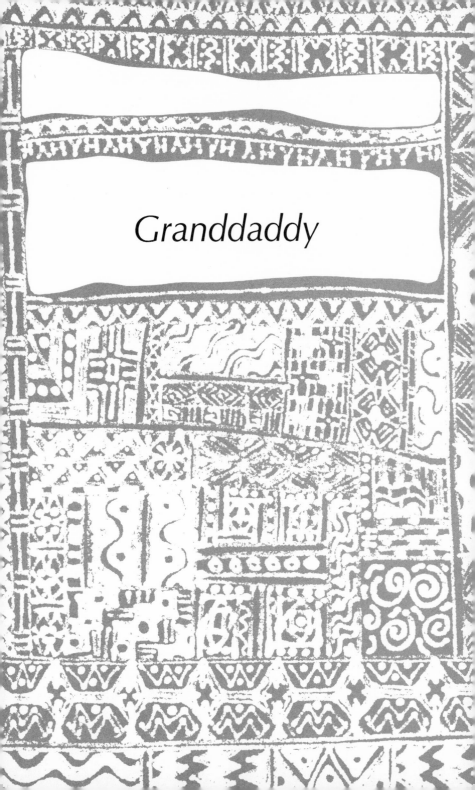

# *Granddaddy*

*I* drove along a road in southern Georgia. It was a night without a moon. Beyond the pine trees and farmland I could see fire in the distance. Farmers had torched their fields to clear the earth for planting. Bark and grass smoldered at the edge of the road. I saw a tall pine ablaze, and I could not suppress the thought of a burning cross as I drove to the house of the man who killed my grandfather twenty-three years ago.

I had heard the tale all of my life: Drunken white boys drag racing through a small southern town in 1960 had killed my granddaddy. Nobody, I was told, knew their names. Nobody, I was told, knew what happened to them. Things were hushed up. Those were the rumors. What everyone knew was this: Granddaddy was a black doctor in Bainbridge, Georgia. Late on the night of October 30 his phone rang. It was an emergency. A patient was gravely ill. Granddaddy left his home in his robe and pajamas, drove to the small infirmary he ran in town and treated his patient. As he was returning home, a car collided with his. My grandfather was thrown to the pavement. His ribs were broken; his skull was cracked.

Several hours later, the telephone call came to my parents' apartment in Harlem. Granddaddy was dead.

During my childhood, my grandfather was the only adult male I remember openly loving me. Yet, oddly, I seemed unable to absorb the meaning of his death. I felt no grief. Nineteen sixty had been filled with confusing events that disturbed the calm childhood I had known. The distant and accidental violence that took my grandfather's life could not compete with the psychological terror that had begun to engulf my own. The year my grandfather died, my own father returned, and I began to sleep each night with a knife under my pillow.

As I grew older, my grandfather assumed mythic proportions in my imagination. Even in absence, he filled my room like music and watched over me when I was fearful. His fantasized presence diverted thoughts of my father's drunken rages. With age, my fantasizing ceased, the image of my grandfather faded. What lingered was the memory of his caress, the pain of something missing in my life, wrenched away by reckless white youths. I had a growing sense—the beginning of an inevitable comprehension—that this society deals blacks a disproportionate share of pain and denial.

With time, I felt compelled to find out what really happened in Bainbridge that night in 1960.

My family wasn't much help. My stepgrandmother, Madelyn, had suffered a nervous breakdown after the accident and to this day is unyielding in her refusal to discuss it. "It's been twenty-three years," she says. "It took me a long time to get past that. I don't want to open old wounds."

She also feared that, if I stirred things up, "they might desecrate" my granddaddy's grave. If she still held such fears after so much time, I needed no other reason to return to Bainbridge, and so I did.

Black people in Bainbridge had told me my grandfather was buried in Pineview Cemetery. "It's the black cemetery in the

# Granddaddy

white part of town," said Anne Smith, seventy-eight, an elegant, retired schoolteacher. Granddaddy had delivered her baby. "The white cemetery is in the black part of town," she said.

I headed for the white part of town.

The streets were unfamiliar. I had only been to Bainbridge twice before, in 1957 and 1958.

Mama and I had flown to Tallahassee from New York City. Granddaddy had picked us up and driven the forty-two miles north to Bainbridge, Georgia's "first inland port," population 12,714, then. The town lies in the southwest corner of the state, north of Attapulgus, south of Camilla.

My grandfather had moved there in 1935 after his residency at Brewster Hospital in Jacksonville, Florida. Shortly before, he'd divorced my Jamaican-born grandmother, Ruby Duncombe Lord, to marry Madelyn Parsons, a much younger woman. Ruby never had a kind word to say about Granddaddy. Their marital problems were myriad, but among them was her refusal to move to the Jim Crow South from New York. "I'll not step aside for any white people," she boldly claimed. What she really felt, I suspect, was justifiable fear of a life filled with terrorism. But Bainbridge needed a black doctor, so Granddaddy went.

I spent two summers with my grandfather, and a few holidays. I was about four the first time we met, and properly outfitted for the occasion in a brilliant yellow, silk- and- satin-trimmed peignoir. I believed myself devastating. But the straps kept slipping. The sleeves kept sliding. I didn't care. Granddaddy hugged me and chased me in circles around the house till we fell down laughing on the floor.

"Oh, Granddaddy, I don't feel so well," I'd tease.

"We can't have that," he'd say, then run and get his black bag and pretend to prepare an injection.

"No, no. I'm fine, Grandpa." He'd chase me again.

"Sure you're fine now?"

"I'm sure." I squealed and ran myself silly. He'd catch me, hug me and tickle me to tears.

Now I was searching for his grave.

The weather was windy, cold, very gray. In the car, outside the cemetery, I sat searching for my sunglasses. I kept fumbling for them, in my purse, under the seat. I had not cried once.

It was my third day in town. I had talked to dozens of people who knew him, trying to reconstruct his life and death. I wanted to be professionally detached, unemotional. I cursed the missing sunglasses.

Thirteen minutes later I gave up and stepped out of the rented car.

I began walking around the southern rim of the graveyard. His would be a big tombstone, I was sure.

*"Was he good?" repeated L.H.B. Foote incredulously. "One of the best. He never stopped trying to learn medicine and that makes any doctor good." Leonard Hobson Buchanan Foote, M.D., did not look his eighty-five years. We had sat in his Tallahassee home on the Florida A&M University campus. For forty years he had been the director of student medical services there. He had been one of my grandfather's closest friends.*

*They entered Howard University the same year. "The freshman class of 1918," Foote said. The year before, my grandfather had immigrated to the United States from Georgetown, Guyana, then a British colony.*

*"I was just a boy from Maryland," Foote said, "born and reared just north of Baltimore." Granddaddy, he recalled, "was tall, slender, a nice-looking young colored man with a foreign accent. I'd say, 'Man, I can't understand you. What are you saying?' He'd say, 'You just listen real good. I speak the King's English.' I said, 'What king?' He said, 'The King of England.' 'You're one of those West Indians, huh?'*

# Granddaddy

'Yeah, what's wrong with that?' 'Not a thing,' I said. 'Welcome here, brother.'

"I felt like I had lost a brother when he died. He had a lot of whites who were his friends, some of them were his patients."

But, he said, Granddaddy had been the object of some resentment. There are, explained Foote, "three things that the southern white man has tried over the years to keep out of the hands of blacks—education, money and social rank. Your grandfather had all that."

As I walked to the western edge of the graveyard, I heard voices nearby. Several houses lined the western perimeter of the cemetery. I stared at the windows looking out on the tombstones.

"Rumor was, one of the boys in the car could look out of his kitchen window and see Daddy's grave," my aunt Earlyne had told me.

I searched for nearly an hour. Finally, I reached the north end. About fifty feet ahead of me I spotted a gray marble headstone.

I stepped closer to the tombstone, a solitary monument in a twenty-foot-square plot. It was the biggest headstone in the cemetery: THE FAMILY OF DR. E A R LORD.

I stared standing in the cold. I wiped my nose. In the crevice of the chiseled letters that formed the word "of," dirt and rain had left a sooty streak. It was the only smudge on the stone. Unconsciously, I leaned forward and began to wipe the stain with the pink Kleenex in my hand. I rubbed hard against the marble. The tissue frayed and disintegrated in the wind.

On the slab of marble that covered his grave was the symbol of the medical profession, the caduceus with its entwined serpents on a winged staff. Engraved in the stone was his full name: EDWARD ADOLPHUS RUFUS LORD SR. M.D.

They called him Earl Lord for short. He was born July 26,

1897, in Georgetown, Guyana. He died October 30, 1960, in Bainbridge, Georgia.

"Wasn't from around here," Bernice Busbee drawled. The man across from her stood gnomelike behind the rocking chair in his office, smiled like Puck and softly proclaimed himself "the oldest living white person in Bainbridge." Then Mortimer Alfred Ehrlich, M.D., eighty-nine, sat down and rocked.

He was retired. As a younger man Dr. Ehrlich had often come to my grandfather's infirmary to help with surgery. He was one of the few whites in Bainbridge whom my family thought of as a genuine friend.

I told him only that I was a newspaper reporter doing a story about small-town doctors; I wanted him to speak freely. Then I asked him about Dr. Lord.

Dr. Ehrlich regarded me thoughtfully.

"I don't want to talk bad of the dead," he said. I switched off the tape recorder and smiled my encouragement.

"He was a bad man," Ehrlich finally said. The old chair groaned with each rock.

"Blacks didn't like him either," Busbee offered. She had been Ehrlich's receptionist for thirty-one years. Now they spent their days making quilts for comfort when it's cold. "He was an undermining, sneaky fellow," she said. "He tried to bring the NAACP in here."

"Lord was for integration," Ehrlich elaborated.

"He just didn't fit in," she said. "Didn't understand the people. Didn't know our ways. We were all glad when he was gone."

My smile was beginning to ache.

"If he hadn't been killed in the accident, he would have been shot," Ehrlich said. "Better he was killed that way so we didn't have the bother of a trial for whoever shot him."

# Granddaddy

We spoke for a few more minutes. Then I rose to leave and shake his hand. He offered the tips of his fingers.

I left him rocking.

That old white southerners would have believed that the NAACP was subversive, and condemned my grandfather for belonging to it, did not surprise me. That my grandfather was political at all did.

I had thought my family in Bainbridge to be insulated, apolitical members of the southern black bourgeoisie under segregation. I recall going to a movie theater with my uncle Paul and my aunt Pat, the youngest of the five children Granddaddy had with Madelyn. I wandered to the "wrong" side of the theater lobby to read the posters advertising the coming attractions.

*"No, come here," Aunt Pat said, tugging me gently.*

*"Why?" I boomed, pulling her to where I wanted to be.*

*"You just can't," Uncle Paul told me with no further explanation. He was tall, handsome and dark brown like Granddaddy, while Aunt Pat was so pale she could have gone into the "whites only" section of the theater unnoticed. But I recall no signs that announced the Jim Crow seating plan. I had never heard of him, and my aunt had to put a hand over my mouth to quiet my protests from the balcony.*

*"Why are we up here? Why can't we sit downstairs?"*

*I remembered that night in the theater when I called Aunt Earlyne to tell her I was going back to Bainbridge.*

*"We always grew up so secure," she insisted. "We could just walk into any store and say 'Charge it.' " As she spoke, I envisioned the delicate string of pearls, my first and only, that she sent to me when I was just a toddler. The Lords, she said, could take clothes out of a store on approval at any time. This was when most southern blacks weren't allowed to try on a pair of shoes. You bought them and suffered if they didn't fit. "We never really felt any open hostility toward us," she mused. "But it was always something you knew was there. You*

*knew how far you could go in raising an issue. Some things you could get away with. Others, you knew you could not. It was a KKK city and KKK members ran it along with a few politicians from the town's first families."*

I would find out later that my grandfather had spoken out for equal pay for black and white teachers in Bainbridge long before the 1954 U.S. Supreme Court ruled that separate could not be equal. He wanted black and white students to use the same textbooks. He wanted black students to ride buses, not walk miles to school.

"All of these inequities were addressed by Dr. Lord," said S. B. Bryant, the retired assistant principal of Hutto High, once all black. Now it is an integrated junior high school. He is seventy-one and blind.

"No one liked the disparities, but there were those who sat supinely by and took it. And there were those, like Dr. Lord, who were concerned." As schoolteachers, "we couldn't openly contribute to the NAACP and keep our jobs.

"Dr. Lord, however, *stayed* in the superintendent's office pleading the cause, so much so that when they got ready to name the swimming pool, it was named after him."

It was the only city-owned swimming facility that allowed blacks. It wasn't integrated until 1970.

There was also a street named after him, in the black part of town. Lord Avenue. It's still there. Still in the black part of town.

Granddaddy's name is still painted on the window of the infirmary he once ran. It is a flophouse now.

Bainbridge seemed a little town locked in time.

The downtown streets were mostly vacant, empty of traffic. An old white man sat on a bench, muttering to himself in front of the gazebo.

# Granddaddy

The city built the latticed structure a few years ago. In Chamber of Commerce literature costumed southern belles adorn it, but on this day no one was there but the self-absorbed old man and some goldfish. The fish swam in a pool at the base of a statue of a Confederate soldier. Along the marble rim of the pool in gold was: BAINBRIDGE, INCORPORATED 1829.

I felt like an alien there.

I was born in Brooklyn, the daughter of a Marxist historian and a nurse. I had studied most of my life to be a musician, an opera singer. In the 1970s I embraced what was considered to be radical black politics. I rejected my slave name for an African one. I began to wear only traditional African clothes. I abandoned classical music because it was incompatible with my newly aroused sense of cultural identity. In time I would come to see that black nationalism almost inevitably leads to a kind of cultural chauvinism indistinguishable from racism, the very thing I thought I was fighting.

But no moderation of my political views could make me tolerate the stifling atmosphere of Bainbridge. On my first day in town I spoke with some of the city's young blacks. They spoke with bitterness about the professional opportunities denied them in their hometown. And they laughed dryly at the social outlets Bainbridge offered them: Skatetown, the roller rink, its six nights of rock set aside for soul on Sundays, the unspoken invitation that let blacks know that night—and only that night—was theirs. Meanwhile, their white counterparts got to go to the country club, to which no black belonged. And like the generations of blacks who lived there during and before my grandfather's day, they all said: What do you do if you're black in Bainbridge and you've got ambition? Go to Tallahassee.

*"Some nights, a chilling silence would fall on the town," my mother told me, recalling one particularly stark image she maintained of Bainbridge. "It was that time of evening after supper, when the dishes were*

*done and families would gather in the parlor before bed." It seemed as though the town had gasped, held its breath, then minutes later released it with a shudder, she said. "The next morning, word would come that someone had been lynched."*

As I walked through the town, I imagined how much more cruel a place it was when my grandfather, elegant and worldly, lived and died there.

I remembered his house on Planter Street in the way a child recalls a beautiful, festive dream. All the room! Lots of space to dance whenever music played; music that poured down on me from above. Granddaddy had installed an elaborate music system with speakers in the ceiling of each room.

In the front of the house was a circular driveway that led to the porch. A dark blue canopy stretched from the front door to the street, to protect guests from inclement weather. Art deco glass bricks framed the windows in each room. A glass brick bar stood on the circular patio in the rear of the house. Four giant white columns grandly marked the boundaries of his property.

What an impertinence that house must have been for a black man in Bainbridge in 1942.

I wondered how many whites in Bainbridge had mourned his death? Who among them would have stepped forward to demand punishment for his killers?

How do you unlock a twenty-three-year-old mystery? Without much hope, I visited the newspaper, the *Bainbridge Post-Searchlight*, published twice weekly, to see if their morgue contained any reference to my grandfather's death, any leads I could follow. I expected to find nothing, but I was wrong.

On the front page, November 3, 1960, where a week later the newspaper would report the election of John F. Kennedy, was a four-paragraph story:

"Dr. E.A.R. Lord, well known colored physician, died early

# Granddaddy

Sunday . . ." My eyes raced down the column. ". . . enroute to Memorial Hospital of injuries sustained . . . The accident, according to Bainbridge police officers, occurred . . . intersection of Planter and Scott . . .

"Dr. Lord, driving a '53 Ford . . . The other vehicle . . . '57 Dodge driven by . . ."

Nothing quite registered. I had always been told no one ever found out who did it, that the killer had been protected by the white establishment.

But here was his name, on the front page.

John Lawrence Harper, twenty-two.

I jumped for the phone book. Harper wasn't listed, but I felt it didn't matter. If he was still alive, I knew I could find him.

And ask him—what?

I needed more information before I could confront him. How had the accident happened? Was he drunk? If his name was known, might he even have been punished?

With a name, I thought I could find these things out. I hurried across the street to the courthouse.

The files for 1960 showed that John Lawrence Harper had never been charged with a crime. Expecting nothing, I checked the civil court records. A clerk pulled the dockets for the 1960–61 term for me. There was a case styled *Madelyn P. Lord* vs. *John Lawrence Harper.*

I stared at the page in disbelief.

My grandmother, who had been silent all these years, had not only known the identity of the driver, but sued for damages in 1961. One hundred thousand dollars in damages.

In the file, I found a police report. Under the "apparent cause of accident," it said Harper was "exceeding lawful speed." There was no mention of alcohol.

The case had gone to trial. Harper had alleged the accident was my grandfather's fault; my grandmother had claimed Harper was to blame. On May 5, 1961, a jury had reached a verdict: six thousand dollars for Madelyn Lord.

I called my aunt Earlyne. She was shocked. She knew nothing about a civil suit. She only knew her mother never tried to press any criminal charges both because she was so "traumatized" by Granddaddy's death and because of "politics." It was a Klan town, she reminded me.

But if my grandmother was so traumatized, how did she find the wherewithal to proceed with a civil suit?

Her friends pressed her to do it, said Anne Smith, the retired teacher who told me where to find my grandfather's grave. My grandmother was so upset, she recounted, she let strangers take my grandfather's car away.

My aunt recalled the same story. "Someone took it after the accident, fixed it up and was driving around town in it."

After Granddaddy died, Smith said, my grandma Madelyn was still going into stores charging things for which she could not pay. "I'd go to the house, get the jewelry and have to take it back to the store," Smith said. My grandmother lived in a daze, she told me.

I knew the fog had lifted for my grandmother, but not the fear.

I searched for transcripts of the trial. If they ever existed, they were gone. All that was left, except for routine paperwork, was the list of jurors.

They would be all white. Blacks weren't called for jury duty in Bainbridge, Georgia, in 1961. How would these jurors react to me, a black woman from Miami, on their doorstep asking questions about the local boy who had killed her grandfather?

I wanted the truth, and in this particular town complete honesty didn't seem to be the way to get it. As with Dr. Ehrlich, I decided not to mention I was Dr. Lord's granddaughter. Further, I decided to interview the jurors by telephone. I did not want them to know I was black.

I wanted to be fair. But more important, I wanted the truth.

I wanted to know why Granddaddy died.

Juror James F. Steadham, now seventy-four:

"It was the middle of the night," he remembered. "Lord was half drunk, half asleep. . . . The boys had gone out to the Dog and Gun Club and I think they were about half drunk and they just run together . . ." How good was his memory? The police report made no allegations about alcohol. There was no mention of a blood test for Harper or an autopsy report for my grand-father. I thought it unlikely that Granddaddy had been drinking. He had been aroused from bed by a phone call, had driven to the infirmary and treated a patient. Would he have stopped at a bar on the way home in his pajamas?

I asked Steadham if he knew Dr. Lord.

"Yeah, I just knew him when I saw him. He was a nigger and . . . wasn't much association between white and niggers at that time. I had nigger friends that I think just about as much of as white friends."

But "Lord," he said, "was kinda arrogant. Sooner or later somebody would have shot him. He didn't understand the peo-ple here. . . . Bainbridge was a good town to live in for both black and white. He just didn't get along too well with the public. I think he must of come in from the North."

How, I asked him, was the six-thousand-dollar figure arrived at? It seemed a small sum to me even for 1961.

"We kicked that around a bit. Money was scarce and hard to get," he said. He said he thought the award was just. The jury had discussed it, he said, and one juror had pointed out:

" 'Never saw a hundred-thousand-dollar nigger.' "

In the next few days I would reach four other jurors,

bridge police chief James "Jabbo" Duke, the lawyer who had represented my grandmother in the suit, the former police officer who had investigated the accident, the former district attorney.

No one agreed on anything.

Two of the four jurors I could still find said they remembered nothing of the case. The third said my grandfather had been at fault. The fourth said Harper had been at fault. My grandmother's former lawyer remembered almost nothing about the case, nor did the cop on the scene ("I can hardly remember what happened a week ago"). Chief Duke was also hazy, but he remembered my grandfather well. He said he had been well respected by blacks and whites alike, and a fine doctor.

It was the first kind word about my grandfather that I had heard from a white person, but I could not shake off a skepticism about his sincerity. He hadn't offered his hand to me when we met or parted, either; nor had I offered mine to him.

The police accident report listed two witnesses, though it didn't specify how they happened to be involved. One had left Bainbridge. "That's my son you're talking about," said Benson Woodbery's mother. "No one knows where he is. When the accident happened, he was living with his grandmother." Last she heard, he was living in Florida. ". . . But he's just the kind that drifts," the mother said.

The other witness was Lee Parker, Bainbridge's postmaster. I called him.

"I don't know why they would have my name as a witness. I passed by the accident after it happened. Maybe a half hour, an hour later. Yes, I knew Larry Harper. I grew up in Bainbridge. His father still lives here," Parker told me. The father's name was C. E. Harper.

A short, plump, white-haired man answered the door. He looked like a man perpetually on the verge of telling a joke. In his living room he pointed to a plaster of paris bust swathed with red cloth. He undraped it. It was a woman with cascading, shoulder-length hair and bare breasts big enough to suckle a nation. He laughed. His wife covered it again.

The father of the man who had killed my grandfather was sixty-nine. He seemed genuinely friendly, but clearly uncomfortable. Again, I told him only that I was a reporter writing about small-town doctors, and that during my interviews, Earl Lord's name had been mentioned repeatedly as a physician who'd had some influence in Bainbridge. I asked about Dr. Lord's death.

He said he didn't remember much about the accident. I asked if he knew of any witnesses.

"Lee Parker was in the car with Larry," he volunteered.

Lee Parker. The man who'd been listed as a witness to the accident but denied knowing anything about it. What was he hiding?

I said nothing.

Harper's wife, Estelle, sat staring at the black reporter and white photographer in her living room.

"This isn't going to stir up any racial thing?" Harper asked. He looked genuinely concerned.

"I used to sell insurance, you know," he went on. "I have lots of black friends. Always got along well. I called Larry to tell him you were coming. He wasn't home. He's in Albany, Georgia, now, selling insurance.

"This is not going to stir up a black-white thing?" he asked again. "I know Larry really hated it when it happened," the father assured me.

Perhaps he really did, I thought, looking at the genial man who was his father, a man who had never been deliberately unkind to a black person in his life, probably. Perhaps his son was like him. Probably. Perhaps.

I went back to my motel room and telephoned John Lawrence Harper in Albany.

I kept rehearsing my tone of voice—calm, businesslike, detached. I was trying to keep the nerves and anger out.

His voice was pleasant, youthful. I said that in the course of my story on doctors I had become interested in Dr. Lord, and that I was trying to reconstruct the events of his life and the accident that caused his death.

"So . . . what do you want from me?"

"I'm trying to find out what happened," I told him.

"I wouldn't even be interested, it happened so long ago."

I asked if he ever thought about the accident.

"Naw," he said. "The case that happened then was then. I had a lot of feelings then, none now."

I told him there are no official records explaining what actually happened.

"Yeah, probably never will be either, will it?" he tossed out cockily. ". . . Probably wasn't important enough to."

I stiffened. "Someone *did* die."

"So, people die in accidents every day."

"What were the circumstances?" I repeated.

"Oh, gosh, it could be a million circumstances. . . . Good heavens . . ."

There was a click. The line went dead. I called back.

"I thought we were through. It's so irrelevant now. You think there's some mystery here to be unwound. I was in a car. Another man was in a car. We met under a red light . . ."

"Your father . . . told me that Mr. Parker was in the car with you."

"He remembers more about it than I do."

"Why did Mr. Parker say he wasn't involved then?"

"I'm sure he looks back on that thing . . ." He paused. "It

was a trying experience for all of us. I don't imagine he *wanted* to be involved at the time, and his feelings, probably, when you called him, came back. He probably doesn't recollect the event hardly either.

"There was nobody in the car with me," he said.

"So your father was incorrect?"

"Ah, probably so if he said that."

"So Mr. Parker was not there?"

"Uh, when did you talk to Daddy, today?"

"Yes."

"Yeah, he remembers more about it than I do," Harper repeated sarcastically.

He was understandably defensive, shaken to have an incident half his lifetime old resurrected. That was the reason for the cockiness, the sarcasm, I tried to convince myself. I knew I was upsetting him badly but still I pressed him.

"Do you go to bed with a clear conscience about this?"

"Clear conscience—now wait a minute . . ." He raised his voice for the first time. "You went too far there. That thing was cleared up twenty-three years ago and you're asking me something about a conscience. Hey, don't call me anymore." He hung up.

I sat there on the bed of my motel room, trembling. Around me were all my pens and notebooks, all the trappings of the dispassionate journalist.

No, Harper was wrong. It was not "cleared up."

I had to see him in person.

We drove past one-blink-and-gone towns built around railroad tracks, grazing cows and pecan orchards to get to Albany. It was close to dusk when we arrived. The only gas station open downtown had no maps of the city. I found Harper's address in an old phone book at the service station and asked for directions. We got sent to an area of dilapidated shacks near an old railroad station. It was the wrong place.

We turned back toward town and checked into a Holiday Inn. A more recent telephone directory had a different address.

The house was in a well-to-do subdivision with nicely trimmed lawns and lamps at the front door. No lights were on at Harper's address. It was 9:10 P.M. We drove around and returned twenty minutes later. The house was still dark. The photographer stayed in the car while I got out to look closer. The house was empty, recently vacated, it appeared. Newspapers were still in the driveway.

Frustrated, I returned to the motel and dialed information. The operator gave me the same telephone number for Harper that was listed in the current phone directory, but at another address. I resorted to a cab company for directions.

We drove miles past the city limits unable to find it. The absent moon and clouds made the night sky seem opaque. The sudden flicker of light in the woods was startling. I'd never seen torched farmland before. The deeper we drove into the countryside, the more widespread the flames. The fields the farmers set afire posed no danger on the damp earth. It was the glowing branches at the road's edge, overlapping like a cross, that made me shudder . . . drift . . . into a psychic film noir replay of the past twenty-three years.

We had driven twenty miles and were lost. We turned back. Fifteen miles toward town, I spotted it, Harper's street, just before a railroad crossing. The house was in a tract of modest single-family homes and duplexes. It was midnight. We'd have to return in the morning.

We went back to the Holiday Inn. I drank a shot of cognac and smoked half a pack of cigarettes. I don't care much for liquor. I don't smoke.

# Granddaddy

At 7:40 A.M., I stepped from my car into the rain at the home of the man I wanted to see. The photographer remained in the car. We knew a camera would make things more difficult.

The house was divided into two apartments. Harper's was on the left. The heels of my black pumps sank in the red mud that covered what should have been a lawn. I entered a dark foyer and pressed the bell. Gloria Harper, his wife, answered the door. I told her my name and gave her my card.

"We have nothing to say to you." She was five feet two inches at most, plump, had brown hair and wore glasses. She pulled the floor-length robe tighter around her.

I told her only her husband could tell me what happened the night of the accident. She stared at me as I stood in the dimly lit hallway dressed all in black, my hands in my pockets, the collar of my coat turned toward my beige cheeks.

"My husband's getting dressed for work. He has nothing to say to you." She shut the door in my face. I stood there for a few moments, breathed deeply, then pressed the bell again.

"Look, I told you—"

I interrupted. I told her what I had heard about the accident.

She stood there framed by the open door. A young boy walked behind her and stood slightly to her left. He was not more than sixteen, bare-chested and dressed in jeans. His hair looked ash blond. One could not be sure in the pale light. But his face was clearly beautiful. He looked pained and perplexed at my presence.

"I'd like to hear your husband's version of what happened."

"He has nothing to tell you," she said.

"Let *him* tell me that, Mrs. Harper." Then I told them. "I'm not interested just as a reporter," I said. "I am Dr. Lord's granddaughter."

"I knew it," Harper exclaimed. He had been standing at the side of the door, out of sight, listening.

29

He had on a yellow shirt and tan slacks and wore glasses. He looked older than forty-five. Perhaps because his hair was so white. His wife and son formed a zigzag line of defense in front of him.

"I knew it had to be someone from the family," he said excitedly. His hands were stiffly at his sides. He stared at me from behind his child. I realized my stance may have looked threatening. I took my hands out of my pockets.

"You just stay right there," the wife said. "We're calling the police."

"I knew it, I knew it . . ." Harper kept saying. I heard him pick up the phone. The wife shut the door in my face again. I stood there for a moment, wondering what would happen to me if I stayed to be taken to some small southern city jail. I left.

We drove past groves of nut trees in the drizzling rain and away from Albany. The landscape and the graying light pushed thoughts of John Lawrence Harper from my mind. And my heart slowed, enough for me to think and take stock of what had happened.

I had stood on a man's doorstep and humiliated him in front of his wife and child.

For what? What had he done?

Twenty-three years ago he had the misfortune to be in an auto accident that claimed a life.

The rumors had been wrong. There was no evidence of drag racing, none I could find. If there had been a cover-up, it had been pretty inept. Harper's name was front-page news in the local paper. If there had been an injustice, hadn't it been mitigated by a six-thousand-dollar award by a white jury to a black woman?

Despite the pain that induced it, hadn't my grandmother's

silence for twenty-three years kept alive in my family a hurtful distortion?

And yet I felt like screaming. Because nothing was resolved, nothing was settled. Absolutely nothing.

I came to Bainbridge, Georgia, hoping to find and expose a killer who had been protected by a white racist society for twenty-three years. That, or something else: to discover that the man who killed Granddaddy had been punished, and that he and the people of his town, whites and blacks, had mourned the loss of a man such as E.A.R. Lord.

But I found neither thing. I found no clear-cut guilt or innocence, nor did I find my grandfather warmly remembered.

In Bainbridge, Georgia, 1983, I found a town that had changed very little in the last twenty-three years, one that had entered this quarter century only reluctantly, dragged by the courts, pouting, without guilt. Yes, it does have integrated schools and a lone black city councilman. And it named a street after a dead black doctor. But it is still strangled by plantation-style racism: gentle-voiced, genteel whites unabashedly talking of niggers, white people still so contemptuous of blacks that they would not soil their hands by touching mine. There is still a black part of town and a white part of town. A black cemetery and a white cemetery. Skatetown rock on weekdays and Skatetown soul on Sundays. Opportunities for whites, a bus ticket out of town for blacks.

And who is to blame?

I came, tried to find blame, and I failed. I wanted to stay in Bainbridge longer. I wanted to go back once I returned to Miami. With more reporting, I argued, I could find an answer; the truth. My editors said no. Then they suggested that Bill Rose, a white reporter born and raised in the South, try to talk to Harper, just to see if he'd feel less threatened. I agreed.

Harper ran to the men's room in his office building when Rose came to see him and would not talk.

At the paper, we struggled with this story for months, arguing over its point of view and the need to dig deeper. It was the only way to find the truth, I bellowed. Finally, I was compelled to write.

A woman whose family had lived in Bainbridge walked into the newsroom months after my return. She was a Miami writer. She told an editor she had something to tell me. Her uncle had been killed by "rednecks" in the town, she said. They had found him walking in the woods, beat him and left him to die. It was the 1930s, she said; about the time my grandfather came to Bainbridge; about the time my mother remembers the chilling silence that fell on the town some evenings. Her uncle's murder, said the woman, almost destroyed her grandmother's life, contributed to her own mother's mental breakdown. The pain becomes "generational," said Marjorie Klein, whose uncle was a Jew.

There is so much blood on the land, who will ever know The Truth?

And so, as a matter of law and justice, I am compelled to consider the whites of Bainbridge to be innocent: the man who drove the car, the jurors who had "never seen a hundred-thousand-dollar nigger" and awarded six thousand dollars, the white town that did not prosecute.

Yet I cannot.

In the absence of proof of guilt, I need some proof of innocence. Or I am left, against the backdrop of my life and the lives of so many others, to wariness.

Would John Lawrence Harper have been prosecuted had he been black and my grandfather white? Can you really expect me to assume otherwise? On that night in Bainbridge, Georgia, twenty-three years ago, even if just for a moment, did John Lawrence Harper heave a sigh of relief that it was only a black man who had died?

How could I assume otherwise?

I feel the suspicion in me. I feel the hatred creeping up. Those feelings are so powerful, they cannot be extinguished by trustingly extending to the town, to the man, the benefit of a doubt. Trust requires more than a failure to prove guilt; it requires a belief in innocence.

The night my grandfather's skull cracked against the pavement, my grandmother Madelyn flew through the street, her white nightgown, her pale, pale skin streaks of light against the darkness. She tried to push through the crowd, a witness told me months after I returned from Bainbridge. A white cop pushed her back gently. "Don't worry yourself, ma'am," he told her. "It's just a nigger."

Against a backdrop of personal loss, against the evidence of history that fills me with a knowledge of the hateful behavior of whites toward blacks, I see the people of Bainbridge. And I cannot trust them. I cannot absolve them.

Perhaps you will argue that this is intemperate. Perhaps you will call me a racist. I do not think that I am.

But I am weary of the collective amnesia of most white Americans. I am not responsible for what Daddy or Granddaddy did, they say; and as long as they are innocent of perpetuating the evils of the past, they are right. I read history as a child, not fiction. I understand how insidious was the impersonal social system that had coldly denied opportunity to blacks, and seemingly left no one to blame, as if systems do not bear the marks of their creators.

I saw what it did to my father. It helped shatter him, a classical scholar with a doctorate in philosophy and few options for a black intellectual in America in the 1930s. He spent his life writing about liberty denied because of race and class. He spent his life galled that he was confined to traditional Negro colleges, unrecognized as an important scholar by the white academic establishment, his intellect always defined by the parameters of race.

I found him naked and bloated, lying on his apartment floor, dying, an alcoholic in a diabetic coma, the bills from the liquor store stuck in the pages of his books. I was twenty-five and he was sixty-nine, the anger between us unresolved at his death. I am bitter when I think what society denied him and me. And I am bitter when I think of my grandfather, and the white people of Bainbridge.

In going back to Bainbridge I felt I was tracking down a thousand anonymous bigots whose acts would never be known, whose guilt or innocence would never be judged. Men who killed a black man and laughed. Even men who, without malice, killed a black man and sighed, knowing it ultimately did not matter.

When I returned home, my aunt Earlyne told me that if she met Harper today, she would shake his hand. "That's what Daddy would have wanted," she said. "Turn the other cheek. We can't live in this world with hate."

I know no such charity.

I want a thousand anonymous bigots to know that somebody's grandchild might someday knock at their door, too.

*Ruby*

My grandmother must be feeling a lot of holiday good-will. She hasn't thrown a bedpan at a nurse or told a doctor to kiss her derriere since Thanksgiving, and it's almost Christmas. She seems to be adjusting to life in a New York City nursing home at just the time of year I'd expect her to be most recalcitrant. I am worried. She is even speaking kindly of Earl Lord.

"I saw him," she said. In the early morning darkness she looked toward the foot of her bed and there he was.

My uncle, Alex Lord, the spit of Earl, cocked his head, pulled back his chin so it doubled, then squinted at her with one open, disbelieving eye.

"Daddy? Here?"

"Oh yes, right here," she said, patting the bottom right corner of the bed.

"Mama, you got loving on your mind?" he teased, then bit into the sandwich she had failed to eat for lunch.

I sat in a chair opposite them, watching my uncle devour Grandma's food while she stared into space, her back to the wall of windows that framed the East River outside Doctor's Hospital. A medical emergency—a blockage in her intestines—had brought her here from the nursing home ten days earlier.

The growth was nonmalignant and, despite the blockage, better left alone given her age, the doctors said. As she sat upright on the edge of the bed, the windows behind her held a gray, midday sky. A light snow fell steadily, gently pocking the river's surface then vanishing, lost in the poisoned waters. She sat captured in the cityscape, but her mind wandered beyond its dimensions. As it did, her countenance seemed all-knowing, her spoken, splintered thoughts seemed to say the past had been retrieved and made intelligible—to her. She tossed a fragment at no one in particular, "My mother . . . If only I had known . . ." My uncle eyed her; his arms were across his chest. He'd polished off the sandwich. ". . . And he called my name," my grandmother said, her eyes tightly closed.

"Who did?" my uncle goaded.

"Your father," she said firmly.

"You sure, Mama?"

She puffed up defiantly. "Yes," she said, as if it were the answer to all questions for all time. Her head started to move slowly from side to side as she recalled Earl Lord's voice in the twilight. " 'Ruby. Ruby, Ruby.' " Her head began to move like the heaviest frond of a tall palm, bending . . . yielding to a breeze only she perceived. Perhaps it was the warm breath of my grandfather . . . close to her face . . . one night . . . long ago. " 'Ruby.' "

He had hurt her; he had loved her and hurt her. But he *had* loved her, she said, and came to her that morning seeking forgiveness.

I'd never seen my grandmother so . . . so . . . sensuously mellow. Though she was eighty-nine and physically deteriorating, she was mentally razor-sharp and had never done anything that indicated she was out of touch with reality. Perhaps it was the place. She liked it here. Doctor's Hospital was her style. She could look out the window and see Gracie Mansion.

# Ruby

Here she was treated like the privileged woman she still thought herself to be. In this congenial atmosphere of quiet corridors, attentive nurses and a friendly roommate, my grandmother seemed relaxed and open to myriad impulses from her subconscious.

In her East Side nursing home, she usually sat in a chair scowling at the wall in front of her, while her two roommates lay on either side of her dying. Her hatred for that warehouse of decaying flesh was evident from the bedpans she hurled at the nurses and her shouts of "Kiss my ass" to the doctor. But during my periodic phone calls to her from Miami, where I then lived, I had detected a certain resignation. My mother had confirmed this latest change in attitude. But to hear her speak with such obvious longing for my grandfather was most disconcerting. I'd always thought his name was spelled B-A-S-T-A-R-D in her dictionary. He had been long dead and they had been long divorced before that. Between their marriage and his death, there had been a series of adulterous affairs—one of which produced a child who could be my mother's twin, I've been told—followed by his marriage to my grandma Madelyn, a woman nearly fifteen years younger than Ruby and so much lighter she could pass for white (a significant factor to extremely color-conscious West Indians). Maybe the doctors had drugged Ruby and this was the afterglow. I don't know. But I could feel the heat of her memories that day as surely as I'd felt the sting of the wind off the river as I walked toward the hospital to see her.

She spoke to me now but I only half heard. My uncle's teasing had finally broken her reverie and she was issuing instructions for her funeral. It was a constant topic of hers and by now a family joke. "Four flower cars. . . . And no, absolutely no, in-laws in the first car. . . ." I ignored the familiar litany. I hadn't seen her in more than a year and I studied her face now. It sagged. But her light brown skin was still soft as a baby's and wrinkleless. Her nose, with its African fullness and East Indian prominence in profile, was finally "Roman," my uncle Alex used to declare, " 'cause it roamed all over the place." Her wide, brown eyes were still expressive, registering all she saw, but their color now was a milky brown. I looked at her thin lips and remembered the words that rushed past them on late fall days such as these when I was growing up. Her sound broke our sleep long before the dawn.

"Tide and time wait for no man," she'd bellow, rousing the house like a Jamaican drill sergeant if we weren't ready for breakfast by 7:00 A.M. She'd been raucously rattling cake pans in the kitchen since 5:00 A.M. If she was up, you should be up. She wanted that kitchen clear for baking. She had fruitcake orders to fill.

What a pain she was on a Saturday morning. But what a voice to rise to: the island lilt of it, the royal imperiousness of its tone. The sun and the Queen were in every word.

By the time I'd hit the kitchen she was in high gear: burning sugar, dicing currants, pouring out the extra-proof rum— sipping the extra-proof rum. Be aware: The cake my grandmother made bore no resemblance to the pale, dry, maraschino cherry–pocked fruitcakes most Americans know. This was a traditional West Indian fruitcake and an exquisite variation of it at that.

As a little girl and since, I've been to more than a few West Indian celebrations where the host served a dry, crumbling, impotent confection and dared to call it fruitcake. Only good manners prevented me from going *spittooey* on the floor, like some animated cartoon character. Instead, the members of my family would take a bite, control themselves, then exchange smug glances: Nothing like Ruby's, we'd agree telepathically.

# Ruby

What Ruby Hyacinth Duncombe Lord created was the culmination of a months-long ritual. The raisins, the prunes, the currants and the citron were soaked in a half gallon of port wine and a pint of rum for three months in a cool, dark place. Even after the cake was baked, liquor was poured on it regularly to preserve it and keep it moist for months. When you finally bit into a piece, the raisins spat back rum.

On the special occasions the cake was served—holidays, birthdays, weddings—I was often outfitted in some party frock my mother, or one of the West Indian seamstresses on the block, had made. Sometimes a bit of hem or a snap required last-minute adjustments. My grandmother would run for the sewing tin and make the alterations with me still in the dress. Her mending done, the needle and thread poised in her upheld hand, she grabbed my wrist.

"Grandmaaaaaah," I squealed extravagantly. She sucked her teeth at my absurd resistance.

"Stop that noise before I knock you into oblivion. Are you insane? Do you actually wish to walk around in your burial shroud?" she asked incredulously. And then she pricked the inside of my wrist, breaking the spell of death that fell when cloth was sewn on a living soul.

I do not know the origins of the practice. Perhaps it was African, as were many things, I later learned, we did and said without realizing it. But such things were not unusual in that place, at that time.

I lived in a country one Brooklyn block long. It was an insular world of mostly West Indians who dwelled in both stately and sagging brownstones, and the occasional wood house that dotted the street.

Scattered among them were Afro-American immigrants from the South. Most mornings, the elder members of these extended families could be seen sweeping and hosing down the sidewalk in front of their row or wood-frame homes. Many of them had come north during the first great migration of blacks from the South around World War I. They were escaping the neoslavery of the post-Reconstruction period. At the same time, my maternal grandparents were sailing from the Caribbean to the United States, fleeing the social prison of British colonialism.

Many of these early Afro-British and Afro-American migrants had saved enough money to buy homes in this Clinton Hill enclave and the surrounding Fort Greene neighborhood in the 1940s when the area opened up to blacks.

Our landlady, and hairdresser, too—she operated a discreet salon on the ground floor of her 1860 Italianate row house—was from Barbados. For years, beginning with my mother, she rented the tree-shaded second floor of her home to members of my family before they bought houses of their own.

The block's most recent arrivals seemed to live in the one tenement I recall on our street, a sturdy, pre–World War II structure whose communal corridors were as tidy as the foyers in the block's private homes.

Like most immigrants, those on our street seemed to possess a drive, tenacity and pride that often set them apart from their countrymen. The social ravages of northern, urban life had yet to engulf the citizens of St. James Place. And the American century, a little past its midpoint, had not fully become what it is—vulgar and dangerous without respite.

As I prepared to leave this country each morning, boarding the bus to the Adelphi Academy nursery school, the old man hosing down the street would wave to me and say, "Be good now." I do not remember his name, if I ever knew it. The people outside of my immediate family and their intimate circle of friends were of fleeting significance to me then. My first seven years on earth were dominated by island voices, resounding in narrow brownstone parlors where all that was wood was perfumed by lemon oil, and parquet floors glowed with the reflected light of chandeliers. It was here, in this world, that we cut the fruitcake.

"Love doll, come give Mariella a kiss," my brother's god-mother called to me at one of these house parties, extending her arms and jiggling her bosom. She lived across the street and ran a boardinghouse with a crew of mostly male students from Africa, the Middle East and the Caribbean. She was a good friend to my mother and a second grandmother to me. Ruby took her latter status as a personal insult, an offense compounded by Mariella's looks (pretty), size (petite), manner (flirtatious), and age (ten to fifteen years off my grandmother's).

Among her other sins, Mariella was from St. Croix, and her musical accent and speech tended to be as informal and coquettish as Ruby's were imperial and bellicose.

"Y'know," said Mariella, pointing to me, "I raise her since she was this high." She bent down and measured about a foot off the floor. I was five and looked at her strangely. Even then I could figure out she'd probably had too much rum.

Ruby sucked her teeth disgustedly at Mariella's familial claims, and my mother shot her a don't-start-anything glance. Later, I'd hear my grandmother mutter, "Old gypsy pussy," and label anything Mariella said "Anansi story anyway."

"Gypsy pussy" went right over my head at the time, and it took years of repeated hearings—my grandmother sticking the label on any woman she considered flighty—before its meaning dawned on me.

As for "Anansi story," I always thought she was talking about Nancy, some lady I'd never met. I didn't know Anansi was the famed character of West African folklore, the spider who spun tales, his stories still told by the descendants of Africans who'd been brought to Jamaica.

With my two grandmothers in the room—the monarch and

the gypsy—someone offered a toast. All raised their glasses but no one drank before a bit of liquor had been flicked with fingers to the floor. Ruby had already sprinkled spirits over the threshold when my mother moved into the apartment. Both gestures were a blessing and an ancestral offering.

While I did spend a lot of time with Mariella, who had two grandchildren my age, it was Ruby who was waiting for me after a hard half day at nursery school, then kindergarten, then the first and second grades. I'd tarry with my friends at the candy store before coming home, stocking up on red licorice, candy lipsticks and peppermint sticks. But Ruby and the whole block knew when I was approaching home; my voice came around corners before I did. I knew the Hit Parade by heart, a fact that did not always please my grandmother.

"You too forward," she'd call down to me, her voice floating from our kitchen window above the limestone stairs where I'd planted myself with my bag of candy. Elbows on the stoop, legs dangling the length of three stone steps, I ignored my grandmother and kept singing.

*"Oh the wayward wind is a restless wind, a restless wind that yearns to wander, and I was born—"*

"What you know about a wayward wind, child? Come upstairs." I loved the regal lilt of my grandmother's accent, her tickled tone, despite the firmness of her call. But I pretended not to hear.

*"Sixteen tons and whadiya get, another day older and deeper in—"*

"Jill Stacey!" she bellowed, as I began "Blueberry Hill."

Still stretched along the steps, I bent my long neck back, looked toward the sky and saw my grandmother's head sticking out the kitchen window. "Grandma, you want me?" I asked, my scuffed saddle shoes still beating time against the pavement. *"I found my thrill . . ."*

# Ruby

"Eh-eh," Ruby uttered quickly, then sucked her teeth. "Yes, it's you that I want. Come and don't try me. Ya know I old and fricasseed."

"What's fricasseed?"

"It's what you do to a tough old bird like me. Now come," she shouted, pulled her head in, then shut the window.

Most afternoons, after I climbed the stairs, we listened to *Our Gal Sunday* and *Helen Trent* during the waning days of radio melodramas. And when my mother bought a television set, we became equally avid fans of *As the World Turns*. As we stared at the tube, I rubbed my grandmother's thickly callused feet with a pumice stone. It was the ritual that accompanied our afternoon entertainment.

Grandma would put down her washboard, wipe her hands on the skirt of her white apron, then sit with her feet in the basin of hot water I had prepared. These were no longer the feet of a pampered, Creole, island princess. And from my spot on the floor, I could smell the Clorox on her hands.

As I tended her crusty feet, I had only the faintest notion then of what life had been like for her in Jamaica. The details of her past came in fragments over the years—a long snatch from her every now and then, a snippet from my mother, a revelation from a cousin or an aunt.

I'd seen only one picture of her back in Jamaica. It was taken in Kingston, where she was born in 1897, shortly before she came to America, circa 1917. The photograph captured her standing regally erect, her buxom, hourglass figure wrapped in an ankle-length white dress. Her cotton-soft hair was pulled tightly into a bun, stretching her taupish-brown skin taut across her cheekbones.

I've often entertained the idea of putting that picture on a round, ruby-red tin that held my grandmother's fruitcake and selling it. The label would read:

# EVERY GOOD-BYE AIN'T GONE

## DUNCOMBE-LORD

"The World's Finest Traditional West Indian Fruitcake"

You'd have to order it through Bloomingdale's or Neiman-Marcus. Grandma would like that. But the recipe would have to be kept a secret.

When my grandmother came to the United States, she promised her brother, James Vincent Duncombe, that she would never give the coveted formula to anyone outside the family. He was a lawyer and probably realized a mint could be made from these cakes if Ruby ever had the capital and opportunity to go into business. In fact, wealthy Americans for whom she had worked as a housekeeper and cook tried to buy it from her so they could sell it commercially. "Never," she told them. But it wasn't just the pact with her brother. The measure and the manner of her culinary alchemy was one of the few family treasures she still possessed in America. Her middle-class, multiracial background meant next to nothing here. And given the reality of colonial Jamaica, her place of privilege there was severely circumscribed by an odious color-caste system. The island's lighter-hued, mixed-race population may have isolated itself from the black majority, but its members remained second-class citizens under British colonial rule.

There was a gate in front of my grandmother's house in Kingston, she once told me. She was forbidden to go beyond it to play with certain children.

"Why?" I asked her when I was an adult.

Her response was vague but firm. "We just could not."

"What reason did your mother give?"

She looked at me as if I were stupid, then sucked her teeth. "We did not question our parents."

# Ruby

I suspected her lack of candor came from embarrassment. She did not want to admit that color and class differences were the probable reasons she was forbidden to play with the children. In America, she had become a follower of Marcus Garvey. His wife, Amy, had been one of her childhood friends.

Nonetheless, I've always suspected my grandmother of being an ambivalent black nationalist, drawn to the Garveyites because there was no caste to insulate her from the rawness of American racism.

But I can't be certain; she never offered any clear ideological argument for her "Back to Africa" sympathies.

On the one hand, to this day, if she could she would stand for the Queen of England if Elizabeth appeared on TV and the British national anthem were played. She did so when I was growing up. But if you asked her if she wanted to go back to Jamaica, she'd ask you emphatically, "For what? There's nothing in Jamaica I want to go back to."

Otherwise, she did display a certain nationalist consistency. She proudly quoted the King James Bible: "Princes shall come out of Egypt; and Ethiopia shall soon stretch out her hands unto God." She would always say it dramatically, her arms reaching out to me, ending the quote with a booming *"Yes!"*

She joined the African Orthodox Church, too, renouncing her family's Catholicism in the 1930s because the Pope, she said, had blessed the ammunition the Italians used to kill the Ethiopians.

And she made it plain that her father was a Haitian, proudly declaring his complexion "black, black, black," to make a clear distinction between him and the European father of her half sister, Marie.

More about her father I couldn't say. On this matter, Ruby was also curiously vague. In her day, she insisted again, children didn't press their parents about such matters as paternity.

But I do know something about her mother, Alice Dacre Duncombe. My oldest first cousin, Karen, saw a picture of her and described her as a pretty woman with pale, nearly white skin and long dark hair that she wore in two braids, each one draped over a shoulder. Exactly how my great-grandmother Alice managed to own so much property and run her own business, a dry goods store, in the late nineteenth century is a mystery to me. Shopkeeping had long been a common occupation for free men and women of color in Jamaica. But whether she inherited her property from her well-to-do mixed-race and European relatives, or from her husbands, remains a puzzle.

Though I've heard the stories of the servants and the grand house the Duncombes had in Jamaica and have seen some of the exquisite jewelry and silverware they owned, I suspect Ruby was at best shakily middle-class in Kingston. If not, why did her brother, my uncle Vin, have to come to Detroit and work in Henry Ford's factory to make enough money to finish law school? And he chose to stay in the States after receiving his degree, maintaining a marginal law practice under American apartheid in the 1930s, 1940s and 1950s. (His grandchildren did much better. One granddaughter, Beth Duncombe, is part of a flourishing law practice in Detroit. Her sister, Trudy Duncombe Archer, was assistant dean of the Detroit College of Law, where her grandfather got his degree, and is now a district court judge in Michigan. Her husband, Dennis Archer, is Michigan's second black supreme court justice.)

But in early twentieth-century Jamaica, the Duncombe family's position was precarious. They were mixed-race but dominantly African, and the real nonwhite, middle-class power brokers in colonial Jamaica were the East Indians and Chinese.

There couldn't have been many available men in my grandmother's class to choose from. My aunt Rae, confirming this one day, laughed and said, "You think Mama would have come here if they had any prospects for her in Jamaica?"

Fresh from Ellis Island, Ruby joined her brother, my uncle Vin, in Detroit. In the motor city, she met my granddaddy, and pinned her hopes on this soon-to-be physician from Guyana.

Earl Lord defined arrogance. He truly was tall, dark and handsome, the product of a New World mixture of African, English, East Indian and Amer-Indian. The black Lords of the New World were the descendants of a notorious pirate named Sam Lord. He was my great-great-great-grandfather, and you can spend a few nights in his castle if you go to Barbados. The Marriott hotel chain has turned the place into a popular resort hotel.

This pirate, so the story goes (his life was fictionalized in a 1980 novel called *A Regency Rascal* by W. P. Drury), was actually a landlubbing one. With the aid of slaves from his plantation, he lured ships to a nearby reef by hanging lanterns in the coconut trees. Mariners seeing them thought they were the lights of ships anchored in a safe harbor. When the ships ran aground on the shoals, Lord took possession of the cargo, dispatching the sailors who had not drowned.

The castle he had built in Barbados in 1820 was constructed entirely by slave labor. And though he and his wife had only one child that lived, Samuel Lord had twenty children by four enslaved African women. I wish my family knew as much about those anonymous women, one of whom was my great-great-great-grandmother, as they do about this bandit who allegedly stole money entrusted to him by his nieces and nephews and regularly threw his wife into the dungeon till she fled back to England. He returned to England, too, eventually, and died there in 1845.

The black branch of the Lord clan migrated to Guyana toward the end of the last century, and the men, true to the Lord tradition, were tyrannical patriarchs and womanizers. Though my grandfather didn't deviate from that pattern in his youth, he had mellowed considerably, my mother said, by the time I was born.

To this day, I don't know for certain how many children he had, but there were nine "legitimate" ones, as well as my mother's "twin," at last count. Just as Granddaddy was ending years of financial struggle and starting his medical practice, he left the first four of those children and my grandmother to marry Madelyn Parsons. It was the middle of the Depression, and my grandmother was ill prepared to support a family alone—being a foreign dignitary without portfolio here.

But it seems that Earl Lord was not an irresponsible father, just a dictatorial one. He attempted to bring his children to the South, where he'd established his medical practice. But by that time, his first set of offspring were in their teens, and they apparently didn't want to cross the Mason-Dixon line.

Uncle Alex had to drop out of school to support the family. Always a hard worker, he was never without a job. But there are few good jobs any man, especially a black man, can get without a high school diploma.

My aunt Rae, thought to have the brains of the bunch and destined for law school, married too young and spent her working life in dead-end clerical jobs.

Aunt Glo, the youngest, had theatrical aspirations. She decided to be "hep" till she dropped. Her fast life finally made a few newspapers, I understand, the shame of which compelled my mother to move to Brooklyn after college instead of Harlem, where Aunt Glo was the moll of a well-known gangster. Like Thomas Wolfe, I guess my mom thought only the dead knew Brooklyn.

# Ruby

Vivien, my mother, was the only one who escaped the destructive economic and social consequences of my grandfather's absence. She was beautiful, the oldest, very practical and sickly. She went south for the warm weather and lived with Granddaddy while she was in high school. She wanted to be a social worker. Granddaddy wanted her to be a nurse and he made it clear that if he was paying her college tuition, she was going to be a nurse.

Meanwhile, my grandmother was not entirely without resources of her own. She had a good education and spoke with a refined, Afro-British accent. The former was of no particular value in America. But the latter, combined with her color and talent in the kitchen, qualified her as an exotic variation of the colored housekeeper/cook. After moving from Detroit to Washington, D.C., where Granddaddy was enrolled at Howard University, Ruby moved to New York to be with other members of her family. In Greenwich Village, she was welcomed into the homes of doctors and lawyers for a while as head cook and bottle washer. But rich people fall on hard times, too. Grandma was out of work. She and her children went on the relief rolls. To make extra money, she sold her fruitcakes for weddings and holidays.

I never saw my grandmother in a place of her own. Perhaps she could have done more with her life despite the profound and pervasive racism that defined America most of her eighty-nine years. Some of her children seemed to think so. "Spoiled" and "lazy" were words family members often used to describe Ruby. "A con artist," too. As an adult, I have seen my grandmother play both ends against the middle, with cash as the reward. But as a child, I thought she could do no wrong.

When the Oxydol commercial ended the half-hour television drama we'd been watching, I dried her feet and smoothed on the almond-scented lotion we both loved. These concluding actions overlapped seamlessly each day and were ceremoniously sealed by the *clang-clang* of the junk man's belled cart and the *clip-clop* of his horse down St. James Place.

If I recall this time and this place too idyllically, do not blame it on a child's naive rendering of reality, or an adult's wistful longing alone. St. James Place, now part of a landmark district because of its unique architecture and social history, was a haven. My mother sought a more genteel existence and found it there. My recollections are testimony to her determination to insulate me from the certain cruelty that lay just beyond the borders of the block. For contrary to what I felt, the world was a dangerous place for black people.

As I sat tending my grandmother's feet that afternoon in 1957, another year would have to pass before the NAACP could report, for the first time in its history, that there had been *no* lynchings in America. Just an avenue away, my mother couldn't rent an apartment because "No Negroes" were allowed. And I know the block I loved was not held together by culture and class alone. Segregation was the glue, too. It was, after all, just a genteel ghetto.

The junk man's clanging bell became faint music as he rolled south toward Fulton Street. Her feet soothed, my grandmother dozed in the parlor, her elbow propped on the arm of the chair, her chin and jowls resting in the palm of her hand. I crept toward the TV to turn it off. She stirred. "What you doing?" she asked, her voice phlegm-filled and hoarse. "Leave that set alone," she said, squinting at me. "Every shut eye ain't sleep. Every good-bye ain't gone." Indeed, the earth has ears. The night has eyes. "And put *that* in your pipe and smoke it," she instructed.

Several years later, circumstances would compel us to leave St. James Place and I would eventually cease to think of myself as a West Indian first and foremost.

We would buy fifteen-cent tokens, take the A train north of

there to 125th, and move into the apartment my father had rented since the waning days of the Harlem renaissance. There, I would discover a new kind of beauty, a new kind of brilliance, a new kind of pain.

"I have to go, Grandma." I rose to leave her hospital room. She had given me the deed to her burial plot and the handwritten instructions for her funeral. As I put on my coat, she became quite formal, as she was wont to do.

"Thank you so much for coming," she said, then nodded as Queen Victoria might have, indicating she was through with me, and that I might take my leave.

. . . *when he heard Mahalia sing*

Daddy wore boxer shorts when he worked; that's all. He'd sit for hours reading and writing at a long, rectangular table covered with neat stacks of *I. F. Stone's Weekly*, *The Nation*, *The New Republic* and the handwritten pages of his book-in-progress, *The Tolono Station and Beyond*. A Mott's applesauce jar filled with Teacher's Scotch was a constant, and his own forerunner of today's wine coolers was the ever-present chaser: Manischewitz Concord grape wine and ginger ale in a tall green iced-tea glass.

As he sat there, his beer belly weighing down the waistband of his shorts, I'd watch. I don't know if he ever saw me. I hid from him at right angles, it always seemed; this one, the bend of the hallway, a long, dark, L-shaped corridor in our Harlem apartment. I sat cross-legged on the cold linoleum floor. From my hiding place it was at least thirty feet down the long of the L to the living room where my father worked, framed by the doorway. I inspected his seated, six-foot-plus figure through a telescope formed by my forefinger and thumb: bare feet in thonged sandals, long hairy legs that rose toward the notorious shorts—I hated those shorts, wouldn't bring my girlfriends home because of those shorts—breasts that could fill a B cup, and a long neck on which a balding head rested. When he was viewed in isolation, I thought, perhaps I'd see him clearer, know him better.

Daddy was a philosopher, a Marxist historian, an exceptional teacher and a fine tenor. He had the voice to be as great a concert artist as John McCormack, one of his favorites. The obstacles to that career couldn't have been much greater than the ones he actually overcame.

When he received his doctorate from the University of Toronto, he was in his twenties and America was in the third decade of the twentieth century. It was a particularly bad time to be black in America. There was the Depression of course, compelling a lot of white people to live as most blacks always had, but grinding salt into the social and economic wounds of Afro-Americans. There was, additionally, and had been since the post-Reconstruction era, a particularly virulent strain of white racism running amok in the land. Faced with real black political power—bolstered by the support of some poor whites during Reconstruction—the southern white aristocracy had, among other crimes, retaliated with a revived Ku Klux Klan at the end of the nineteenth century and carried its terrorism well into the twentieth with lynchings advertised in papers as white family entertainment. The casual intimacy that had existed between blacks and whites in the South—as long as blacks had no power—gave way to the rigid segregation of Jim Crow. And by the 1890s what was left of black power after Reconstruction was schemed into oblivion by literacy tests, poll taxes and grandfather clauses designed to disenfranchise blacks. The state of Georgia, where my father grew up, established its version of the literacy test in 1908, the year he was born. If you substituted Georgia for Mississippi in a story Lerone Bennett, Jr., relates in *Before the Mayflower*, the main character could easily have been my father:

A black teacher, a graduate of Eton and Harvard, presents

himself to a Mississippi registrar. The teacher is told to read the state constitution and several books. He does. The registrar produces a passage in Greek, which the teacher reads. Then another in Latin. Then other passages in French, German and Spanish, all of which the teacher reads. The registrar finally holds up a page of Chinese characters and asks: "What does this mean?" The teacher replies: "It means you don't want me to vote."

Apocryphal, perhaps, but the tale exemplified enough collective experience that I heard my father tell virtually the same story about a former Morehouse classmate to his buddy, Fred Martin, over the phone one afternoon. He fell into a fit of laughter at the punchline, chuckling hard into a balled fist he held at his mouth. Finally, he said, "Fred, I'll have to call you back," then fell back on the bed, in his boxer shorts, laughing at the ceiling.

When a Harvard law professor, discussing some constitutional issue in a class, singled out my father and said, "In this matter, regarding men of your race—"

"Which race is that?" my father boomed, cutting him off, "the fifty-yard or the hundred?" He claimed he fell out laughing in class after that one, too, but it seemed he always related that particular tale with a sneer at his lips. He'd been at Harvard studying law on a postdoctoral scholarship from 1942 to 1943, the height of the second war waged to make the world safe for traditional, Western imperialism, then being threatened by Hitler and the Japanese.

From the first day my father stepped into a classroom to the last, theories of white racial supremacy were discussed with legitimacy in the halls of academe. In America, social Darwinists, eugenicists, psychologists and anthropologists produced volumes of pseudoscientific literature purporting to prove the racial inferiority of blacks and other people of color on an ascending scale of darkness. But when the Nazis started citing the research done by American scholars as justification for the anti-Semitic tide in Europe, and the consequent extermination of six million Jews, the men and women of the academy had to back-track. The Society for the Psychological Study of Social Issues published a disclaimer in 1938 aimed at the European fascists: ". . . there is no indication that members of any group are rendered incapable by their biological heredity of completely acquiring the culture of the community in which they live."

The group said nothing about American minorities.

In this planetary atmosphere of racialism, Daddy packed up his Ph.D., headed toward the dust others were escaping in the mid-1930s and became the editor of a black newspaper, the *Tulsa Oklahoma Eagle*. He eventually returned to academia and by 1949 was the head of the philosophy department at Morgan State. That's where he met my mother, a nurse many years his junior.

She was teaching health and hygiene classes at the college. She was in the school cafeteria the first time she saw my father. He was the center of attention and laughing raucously, she recalled years later, and with some disdain—the latter sentiment emotional revisionism, I think. Assuming her Mother Superior pose and tone, she said she thought at the time, "Oh my, this man is an exhibitionist." Personally, I think it was roiling hor-mones from the start.

What my father did from 1949 to 1959 is pretty much a mystery to me. My mother—who commits nothing to paper, speaks of the past cryptically and believes all unpleasantries are best kept under a rug—is not very helpful on this score. But from what she's leaked, it seems the first few years of my parents' marriage—a long-distance one—were fine. She was back in Brooklyn and he was away teaching. I guess he was home during summers and holidays before I was born. After,

# . . . *when he heard Mahalia sing*

I vaguely remember his visits. I seem to have regarded him as an unfamiliar and unpleasant uncle.

My mother once let slip that she and my father had taken me to a parade in Brooklyn when I was about three. We were standing near the arch in Grand Army Plaza when he suddenly hauled off and punched my mother in the mouth, with me in her arms. My mother, a very gentle and then-naive woman, said the whole thing left her in a state of shock. My father had never been violent before.

They separated, and I seldom saw my father again until I was seven. That's when my brother was born. My parents reunited, and my father accepted a job as an administrator for the New York State Department of Adult Education.

Anticipating problems because of his past leftist political affiliations, Daddy told my mother not to pack up and move until he had the job for six months. Devoted to the concept of a Daddy-and-Mommy-headed nuclear family, no matter how unstable, she moved us to Albany anyway, giving up our beautiful Brooklyn apartment.

When the Rockefeller administration found out Daddy had been a member of a socialist club, they canned him. In less than a year we were back in the city.

Out of necessity and desire, Daddy decided he wanted to devote his time to teaching young people. He wanted to reach them at a stage in their lives when he felt he could make a difference. He joined the faculty of a Jersey City high school and began teaching journalism, history and English. He also taught English at night to foreign-born students at the City College of New York. His students, I came to learn, loved him. His daughter found it hard to.

After the Albany fiasco, we moved into my father's six-room apartment on 129th Street between Convent Avenue and St. Nicholas Terrace. It was certainly far more spacious than the apartment my mother had on St. James Place. Still well-maintained, the building had been a sprawling abode for rich whites early in the century and a residence for many black professionals during the Harlem renaissance and after. The immediate neighborhood was an attractive, hilly section of Harlem, just a few blocks from City College. All things considered, I hated it. More precisely, I hated my father, so I hated it all.

Our stint in Albany had been my first prolonged encounter with the man, whom I made the mistake of calling Pop—once. He said, "Don't ever call me that again. If you don't like calling me Daddy, you can call me Dr. Moreland."

My mother had deserted me. She had gone to Atlanta with my baby brother to tend my ailing grandma Hattie, my father's mother. Like her son, Hattie Moreland was a diabetic.

Since I hadn't known this man most of my seven years on the planet, and didn't like him much once we were acquainted, I didn't want to stay with him. I asked him if I could stay with a family friend around the corner, Aunt Pearl.

"If she asks you to stay, fine. But don't ask her," he told me. Naturally, I asked her.

When he asked me if I asked her, I hesitated. But I was not a child inclined to lie. So I said, "I don't want to lie. I asked her." I got a beating for that; I got a brutal beating with a belt that left welts and bruises on my legs for months.

I had gotten one other serious spanking in my life, from my mother, and a deserved one. But mostly she believed in talking to her children, not whipping them.

My father, conversely, felt children should be hit for any infraction. Further, they should be seen not heard, speak only when spoken to, and so on. From the day he hit me, the latter became my philosophy, too—toward my father. I never consciously said "I'll never speak to Dr. Marc Marion Moreland again," but in effect, that's what happened. And for ten years,

# . . . when he heard Mahalia sing

I rarely initiated a conversation with my own father. Later he would tell me, "You were a very strange child."

My war of silence was not waged for myself alone. He never beat me a second time. But he was hurting the person I loved most in the world, my mother, and she seemed constitutionally unable to defend herself.

Since my father spent most of his time planted on the commode reading, or at his desk writing his book—a Platonic-Marxist analysis of liberty in the United States from the period of Lincoln's administration to John F. Kennedy's—we had little to say to each other anyway.

But when we did talk, it was to speak of *The Iliad* and *The Odyssey*, the Greek and Roman goddesses and gods. If I would not accept him as father, my curiosity would not let me deny him as teacher.

"Come here, Jill the Pill," he said one day, and told me the story of Persephone, the goddess for whom he'd intended to name me. My mother had wanted to call me Dawn. They settled on Jill Stacey Lord Moreland. I added the Lord, my mother's maiden name, when I was eight. I chucked it all in the end. But long before that, I'd thought my father's desire to name me for so melancholy a figure as Persephone ominous. Though she is the maiden of spring, the season in which I was born, her mythological tales are permeated with sorrow. Taken from her mother, Demeter, to the place beneath the earth where dead souls dwell, she was forced to live there four months of the year with Hades, leaving the earth barren and bleak in her absence.

One day, a question about the nature of truth compelled a thaw in the emotional cold war—nothing less could have. Truth changes, a classmate in the seventh grade had insisted that day. It is constant, I argued, and went to my father for confirmation.

People's perceptions change, I explained to him. New information debunks the lies of the past, but the truth was always there. And I told my father what I had told my mostly white classmates in a Bronx junior high school at the height of the Civil Rights Movement: Black people were always human beings worthy of the same rights other Americans enjoyed, but it took hundreds of years of a slave system that dehumanized the master, as well as the slave, and a social revolution before most white Americans would accept that truth.

My father turned from his worktable, took off his glasses, with their broken right temple piece, and released a long and resonant "Yesssss." And then he spoke to me of a rational cosmos and what Lincoln had to do with Plato. Our philosophical discussion ended, we each went to our separate corners.

When we first moved to the neighborhood, I avoided my father by escaping to the streets. I got beat up every day that summer of 1961. But the initiation was worth it. "This kid's got heart, she keeps coming back for more," announced one of the girls who'd been wiping the concrete in St. Nicholas Park with my face. "You're okay."

This was a much more exciting neighborhood than the one I'd left in Brooklyn. For one thing, the music was better. Every rhythm-and-blues hit could be heard in block-to-block stereo blasting from tiny transistor radios. And many an afternoon I could be found doing the mashed potato, the slop or the twist on the playground till I got cramps in my side from over-exertion.

By all appearances, I was a happy kid. I was, in fact, setting fires in the school bathroom, then running to my third-grade teacher to tell her what I'd found: "A fire in the sink, Mrs. White. I put it out." After the second or third time, she got suspicious and asked if I was setting the fires. "No," I said solemnly. Since I was an otherwise well-behaved, overachieving student, she never pursued the matter when it stopped.

# . . . when he heard Mahalia sing

I must have desperately wanted somebody to know how miserable I was living with my father. But since she had chosen to live with him, I saw no point in telling my mother. Bush-league pyromania having failed, I got ill—all the time. But since I was a sickly kid, no one saw that as a cry for help, either. Rheumatic fever, for instance, is a real, clinical disease. I went into the hospital for a tonsillectomy when I was nine and came out unable to walk. My father never visited me in the hospital. When I came home, I was on crutches.

"Go in the kitchen and get me the hot sauce," he told me the night I returned. I picked up my crutches and hobbled to the kitchen to get it. A few minutes later, he told me to get up and get him a glass of water. I started to get up again. My mother, clenching her jaw and wincing, said, "Sit there. I'll get it." Why she didn't tell the bastard to get up and get it himself instead of sitting there, boorishly chewing his food with eyes closed, as was his custom, was what I wanted to know. But I knew not to make waves. My mother would suffer for it if I did.

As I got older, I turned inward, escaping most afternoons to the cocoon of my blue room and music.

We had brought my piano from St. James Place. But my father had one, too. A beaten, black upright, in the parlor, badly out of tune. But its bench held a treasure of ancient sheet music: Vincent Youmans's "Through the Years" with a picture of Gladys Swarthout on the frayed cover. How I loved the chord changes to "Spring Is Here." And thanks to my father's musical cache, I was the rare eight-year-old who knew the opening verse of "My Funny Valentine": *"Behold the way my fine-feathered friend, his virtue doth parade. Thou knowest not my dim-witted friend, the picture thou hast made . . ."*

I had decided long ago to become a singer and had made a deal with my mother: I'd take boring piano lessons as long as she'd allow me to take singing lessons when I was old enough.

But as I got older, music became less a destined vocation and more an obsession. And in a home where Mommy was a lapsed Catholic and Daddy an atheist, it became God.

But no one close to music is ever far from God. Daddy sat one day in an unaccustomed spot: on the couch, hypnotized by the image and sound emanating from the TV. He still wore only his boxer shorts. I peered around the French doors in his bedroom where I'd been dusting and watched his back as his bare shoulders suddenly heaved. I had to pass him in the parlor to reach the kitchen. As I did, I had to stop. His face was red and wet. Mahalia Jackson was singing "The Lord's Prayer." Oblivious to me, he got up, walked to his bedroom and pulled a clean white hanky out of his dresser drawer and blew his nose. He blew it hard so it honked, and then lay back on his bed and looked at the ceiling.

I put away the dust rag, then walked back to my blue-walled room. There I began years of wondering why an atheist would weep when he heard Mahalia sing.

I ventured from the sanctuary of my blue room one afternoon, walked down the long hallway toward the kitchen, then stopped abruptly at a right angle, the place where the wall turned sharply toward the bathroom. I heard my father in the kitchen several feet away. He was making an ice cream soda, something as forbidden to him as alcohol since he was a diabetic. I heard the clink of the metal spoon against a glass as he sang, *". . . for I lately took a notion for to cross the briny ocean, and I'm off to Philadelphia in the morning."* It was an Irish folk song made famous by John McCormack. I backed up. Too late. He danced across the kitchen threshold in his boxer shorts, stopped when he spotted me in the shadows, then shook his head. He smiled, lifted one leg and both arms in a Jackie Gleason "and away we go" motion, then slid off.

Minutes later he called me. "Jill the Pill, you know this song?"

# . . . when he heard Mahalia sing

I knew all the songs and wrote down the words to "Moon River" for him. Then he asked me to sing it. I was always ready to sing, even for my father.

He sat on the edge of his bed with the lyrics in his hand as I sang. When I finished the final phrase—*"We're after the same rainbow's end, waitin' round the bend, my Huckleberry friend . . ."*—my daddy looked at me and said what others would tell me years later, but with far less poetry, "My girl, you have the celestial vibration." And then he asked me to sing it again . . . told me it was "wonderful. . . ." Then I left him.

For days, maybe weeks, a tense calm would reign in the apartment. Then without warning the hall was filled with harsh voices; he stood in the narrow, shadowy space hitting my mother. "Put it down," he yelled. "Put it down or I'll . . ."

My mother had picked up a lamp in a lame effort to ward off his blows. His shouting had awakened me. I'd been sick in bed with the flu and a high fever. When he saw me open my bedroom door he yelled, "Get back in your room." I did, my body overtaken by tremors and the image of my mother branded on my eyeballs. I swore that I would never let anyone do that to me or anyone else I had the power to help. I had no power to help my mother. And it was an oath with terrible consequences, one I'd have to struggle twenty years to disavow, so that I could permit myself the vulnerability of being human.

I know my father's fury was fueled by his sense of insignificance. He felt himself to be an intellectual giant boxed in by mental midgets. He could be found, Ralph Ellison once told me, pontificating in Harlem barbershops, elucidating the dialogues of Plato to a captive audience of draped men, held prone, a straight-edge razor pressed against their cheeks.

Unlike Ellison, Paul Robeson or Richard Wright, all acquaintances and contemporaries of my father, he was never acknowledged by the dominant culture whose cachet he sought.

Whether he deserved it or not, only a few are ever anointed in an era.

His unreconciled identities—the classic schizophrenia of being black and an American, of which Du Bois wrote, the contradictions of internalizing whole the cultural values of a society that sees you, when it sees you at all, as life in one of its lower forms—stoked his alcoholism.

I know why my father, the Marxist, cried when he heard Mahalia. His rational mind would not accept God, but the spirit of Goodness—for what else is the notion of God?—in her voice could not be denied. Her sound, its cultural resonance, was a reminder of the traditions, the myths that have sustained black people, but from which he was culturally alienated.

And since my father at once critiqued the society that denied him and longed for its approbation, he lived with the pain-filled consciousness of one who knows he is a joke. I think, sometimes, he laughed hardest, so often did I stumble upon him alone, chuckling into his balled fist at some silent, invisible comedian.

When his drunken rages ended, he slept for days, spread out on the bed wearing only his boxer shorts. I watched him on these days, too, daring to come closer, safe in the knowledge Morpheus held him. I examined his face, wondering who he was and why he was. As I watched, he'd lift his head off the pillow, then fall back muttering: "Truth and justice will prevail."

# Who's Bad?

M y cousin Jeffrey looked like Ricky Nelson and always wanted to be the baddest nigger on the block.

"Little girl, come here. What you doin' with that white man?" the black supermarket clerk asked, eyeing me with concern.

"He's not white, that's my cousin," I told him, then ran to catch up with Jeff several aisles away in the Safeway.

"That man wanted to know if I was white, didn't he?" Jeff asked.

"No he didn't," I said, my face as fixed as granite. Jeff looked me straight in the eyes but I didn't blink. I knew nothing made him feel worse than people calling him a white man.

We paid for our groceries—the candy we lifted was in our pockets—then walked up the hill from Amsterdam Avenue to my parents' apartment on Convent and 129th Street.

"You make a really good sandwich," he said, seated at the dining table. I glowed. Jeff didn't often hang out with me. He and my cousin Karen were the oldest grandchildren. I was only number five, and there were a lot of cousins after me, most of them Jeffrey's brothers and sisters. His mother, my aunt Glo, had six kids. It was hard to get any attention in that house when I visited.

An old white man, Mr. Javitz, lived there, too. His family couldn't figure why he chose to spend his last years rooming with my aunt in the heart of Harlem, 116th Street and Seventh Avenue. But I guess Mr. Javitz had the same attitude as my grandmother, who lived there most of the time, as well: "I'm a Harlemite," she boasted, though she'd yet to give up her Jamaican citizenship after more than forty years in America. She loved the neighborhood's insomnia—sirens in the night suggesting a death, a fight, a fire. The constant bustle of humanity hustling to earn a cent below her bedroom window from daylight to dark.

Brooklyn, where I lived most of my life, was just too quiet, my grandmother said. Jeff felt the same way. The lure of the neighborhood streets and the incessant household traffic at my aunt's kept me an afterthought in Jeffrey's world—not to mention my age. But he was in my living room now, eating my hero. I stared at him mutely, watching his jaws move. I was eleven and a half, counting the days till twelve, and he was almost seventeen.

"Where you goin'?" I asked. He stood up and smoothed his puckered shirt.

"I got to go back downtown."

"I can go with you," I told him, rushing to clear his plate from the table.

"I'm not going straight downtown," he said, following me into the kitchen. He washed his hands in the sink, dried them on a paper towel, then quickly inspected his nails. "I got to make a couple of stops first."

"Oh," I said simply. Some girl, I thought. I followed him down the long hallway in our apartment to the front door. He bent down and kissed me softly on the cheek.

"Thanks for the sandwich. See ya later," he said, and ran down the six flights instead of taking the elevator.

# Who's Bad?

It was the usual chaos the next time I saw him at Aunt Glo's.

"Hey man *stoooop*," Jeff screamed as he fell back in the kitchen chair, laughing and yelling at Karen, our oldest cousin. She was pouring a pitcher of grape Kool-Aid over his head. He had put ice down her back.

Aunt Glo, a useless disciplinarian dressed in a muumuu, marched into the kitchen waving a big yellow spoon dangerously close to Jeffrey's head. "What are you guys doing," she yelled, then burst out laughing.

Ducking, Jeff yelled, "Don't hit me. Karen's the one."

Karen—all the younger cousins called her Kay-Kay—was pretty, twenty, and had her arms folded across her infinitesimal bosom. Her smile was villainous. Her nostrils flared and I started giggling uncontrollably.

"What are you laughing at, Linkatara head?" she demanded. Kay-Kay had all sorts of pet names for me.

"Your face," I said weakly, doubled over from laughing.

"You better stop," she warned, "or you know what's gonna happen, you'll be peeing on the floor."

"Oh no she won't, you uncouth children." Aunt Glo giggled. "My niece only urinates. She was the only four-year-old I ever met who said 'urinate' instead of 'pee.' "

Not only that, in my house one didn't have a belly button, or even a navel: "Make sure your umbilicus is clean," my mother instructed at bathtime. She was the oldest of four children. Aunt Glo was the youngest, and a fast-and-high-liver by profession.

She looked down at me knotted on the kitchen linoleum, holding my stomach. "Girl, go to the bathroom."

"Not before me," Karen yelled—also the inheritor of a weak bladder—and dashed past me.

The ruckus didn't seem to faze Mr. Javitz, who was in bed, in the room-with-bath, right off the kitchen. He never complained about the noise. He either slept right through it or was too removed from reality to care. On these visits to Aunt Glo, I'd occasionally see him shuffle out of his room to dish up dinner from the always present pots on the stove. He'd eat in silence then return to his room. He was never unfriendly, just a bent, yellowing man with liver spots and nothing left to say.

How he and Aunt Glo found each other, I don't know. From my mother's perspective, everything about Aunt Glo is best kept hermetically sealed. When it came to her sister, my mother would just shake her head and say, "Going to hell in a chariot."

Like her son, Aunt Glo never wanted people to think she was white. When she shopped in fancy department stores in the 1950s with my brown-skinned mother, white people would approach her *tsk, tsk, tsking*, at their intimate chatter. "You shouldn't be with that colored woman," they'd take my aunt aside and say.

"That's my sister," she'd spit at them.

Aunt Glo had many personas before her expanding figure was relegated to the capacious muumuu she wore in the kitchen that afternoon, waving the big yellow spoon.

St. Patrick's Day, circa 1950, she stepped off a jet wrapped in a white ermine coat, her dyed-green hair framing her naturally alabaster face. My mother looked for a place to hide as this portent of punk approached her in the airport terminal.

I was born too late to hang with Aunt Glo in her salad days. Back then, she'd take Kay-Kay to the Harlem hot spots and let her sip Shirley Temples at the bar. After a night out, she'd get to sleep in Aunt Glo's bed with a mink coat as a quilt.

Aunt Glo had theatrical aspirations. Burl Ives—Burl Ives? right, that's what Kay-Kay told me—was supposed to have thought her very talented. He planned to help her break into show business, Kay-Kay said. Promises, promises. She missed out on stage fame, but her connections with Harlem's underworld in the 1940s and 1950s did generate some notice—a few inches in one of the New York tabloids, family legend has it.

The ignominious publicity compelled my mother to leave Harlem after college and escape to the more genteel borough of Brooklyn.

But we were living in Harlem now, as well, and would for another few years. Living in Harlem kept me straight, kept me balanced, kept me from being culturally denuded. And Aunt Glo was a counterweight—if an extreme one—to my mother's sometimes sterile primness.

My mother's healthier bourgeois values, however, could not be undermined merely by contact with school friends who were thugs-in-the-making, whose mothers hooked, whose fathers ran numbers and worse, or by the general hustling into which certain members of my own family delved. Instead, their influence kept me in touch with the complex realities of a race constantly under siege and endlessly adapting to survive. Between my mother and my extended family of relatives and friends, I had the opportunity to experience, synthesize or discard—very early—the variegated elements of black urban culture.

But Jeffrey never had the consistent guidance I had. He was raised, initially, not by his mother, but by a childless couple old enough to be his grandparents. When his foster mother died, Aunt Glo married his foster father—dead a few years by the time Kay-Kay poured Kool-Aid over Jeffrey's jet black hair.

Jeff jiggled when he laughed, I remember now. He was tall but tended to be pudgy in his teens. The extra flesh added to the altar boy innocence of his face. He was a good Catholic kid who attended parochial school for years. He could take apart and put together anything electrical. He could have been an engineer. But he was a black male surrounded by the hustling life without a counterweight, without a sense of options—and since it was the early sixties, without the reality of many options. He bought into the street life, but because of his looks, the price of admission was made exceedingly high. He looked too much like the enemy, and always had to prove how bad he was.

Jeff was about nineteen, I think, and just out of jail, the last time we had friendly dealings. He was living with Karen's mother in that shattered urban zone called the South Bronx. I lived there, too, off and on for a year because it was closer to the junior high school I was attending—one of the best in the city but far from my Harlem neighborhood.

I was walking from Willis Avenue up 147th Street, past vast, junk-heaped lots, past five-story walk-ups with broken-down front stoops, their iron railings supporting the tight asses of fine, lean Borinquen young men posturing—legs spread open, hands on their balls—and pimple-faced, fatter ones spreading their cheeks on the iron to less effect.

"Pssst pssst, pssst psssst." One called me. I was thirteen now and my flat-chested cousin, Kay-Kay, didn't call me Linkatara anymore. She called me Milk Maid Bessie. The block was full of Borinquen gang members at war with neighboring black gangs. Black people lived on the block, most of them middle-aged and older, but few my age. I ignored them and kept walking. My aunt's building was still a half block away. I passed another occupied stoop.

"Somebody back there wants you," a Borinquen said. "How come you not talking to my friends?" he asked, moving down the steps toward me. Jeffrey suddenly appeared behind him on the stoop.

"Hey Jill," he called to me. He told the men on the steps, "That's my cousin."

"For real?" one of them asked, looking him up and down.

"Yeah," he said.

# Who's Bad?

No one on the street bothered me after that. If someone even tried, another Borinquen would warn him off. "No man, that's Jeff's cousin."

It had gotten to the point where Jeffrey was tired of denying he was white to black people, especially in the joint. Borinquens, as Jeff explained it, assumed he was a spic born in the States who never learned Spanish. They never thought he was a nigger. Out of jail, on the street, bloods told him he was so white why deal with the hassle of being black? Just go on and pass.

I realize Jeffrey didn't look like a redbone, a high yellow or anything else in the nomenclature of color African-Americans use to distinguish our varied complexions. He looked like one of Ozzie and Harriet's kids. But African-Americans are the product of a New World culture: it's been estimated that 80 percent of us are of mixed-race backgrounds. And while U.S. social custom and law have denied that miscegenated reality to perpetuate their own system of apartheid, it wouldn't be the first trick bag black people got hip to and out of.

But more than twenty years after I walked down that South Bronx block, a whole new generation of African-Americans are either hyping or putting down each other based on skin complexion, still perpetuating what Alice Walker calls colorism and what Spike Lee scratched the surface of in his film about color and class conflict among African-Americans, *School Daze*.

And as I write this, Jeffrey's sister—fair-skinned, golden-haired and living in a tenement above crack-infested Harlem—hopes her second baby looks *black, black, black,* 'cause that will validate her in the eyes of other black people, she says. In the meantime, she'd like to give her older son to somebody else to raise, like her mother, Aunt Glo, 'cause he's so *light, light, light . . .*

The judge, preparing to sentence him, put down Jeffrey's arrest record and looked at him from the bench. My cousin was into drugs now and into theft to support his habit. The judge opened his mouth to speak; Jeffrey beat him to it.

"I'd like something corrected, Your Honor. I am not white, I am black," he said, and demanded the racial classification in his records be changed.

"I'm looking right at you and you look white to me," the judge replied.

"That's my grandmother right there," Jeffrey persisted, pointing to the brown woman in the black felt hat. Physical appearance is always a matter of genetic roulette among so mixed a race of people as the descendants of Africans in the New World. Her light brown skin had grayed with age and actually looked the color of taupe now. "If she's black, I'm black," he said with increased belligerence.

The judge changed his racial designation and added a year to his sentence, too.

Jeff seemed straight for a long time after he left the penitentiary. But it didn't last. He started using heroin again. He stole from my mother. He stole from our grandmother. After that, I wouldn't have anything to do with him.

I was cold and formal the last time we spoke. He was staring out the living room window of my aunt's latest apartment when I walked in. The apartment was just a few blocks from the one on Seventh Avenue where Mr. Javitz had roomed. Mr. Javitz was long dead. The building was sprawling, half inhabited, run-down and poised for urban renewal. "Hello, Jeffrey," I said stiffly.

He looked at me sideways, said "Hi," then quickly averted his eyes, fixing his gaze on the cityscape of Harlem rooftops, crumbling crowns on stone, gray prisons.

He did not look like Ricky Nelson anymore. His face was pasty and pocked. His hair was sandy and thin. But he really had stopped using drugs. He had a daughter. Her Borinquen mother was an addict. Jeff didn't want that for his child. He put her in a Catholic school and took a job as superintendent of the tenement where he and Aunt Glo lived.

I talked with my aunt but said nothing to Jeff. When I was ready to leave, I moved toward him to say good-bye, but couldn't. I felt him shrink away from me; I felt him shrinking inside. I simply said, "Bye."

A few months later, his bloated body was found on one of those crumbling Harlem rooftops. Parties to a drug deal gone sour more than a year before had tracked him down and shot him.

I came to New York for the funeral from Miami, where I was working as a journalist. My aunt wanted a big funeral. My mother said there was no money for a big funeral, but she'd do the best she could. She caught a priest on the fly in the funeral home and said, "Father, my nephew is dead and I'd like you to say a few words over him before he's buried." The priest was glad to oblige.

I waited in a vestibule with my other cousins while dozens of friends from Aunt Glo's and Jeff's neighborhood filed into the room where he lay in the alloyed equivalent of a plain pine box. There were no flowers. Thelma, my mother's first cousin, got up from her seat and placed a small bunch of violets on top of the coffin.

"This ain't the type of funeral Jeffrey should have," complained one of his brothers.

"Then you should have paid for it, motherfucker," I told him and walked away. He was peddling drugs and had gotten a younger brother, not even in his teens, busted in a deal.

They carried Aunt Glo in wailing, a person on each side supporting her obese, tented frame. For years she had rarely been seen in public. She almost never left her house.

The priest entered. It was obvious from his slightly quizzical expression and darting eyes that he was trying to figure out what the white man in the coffin had to do with all these very dark and very light and everything-between people.

My mother had told him Jeffrey's full name, and after a few stock religious phrases he began the Hail Mary. ". . . the Lord is with thee, blessed art thou amongst women, and blessed is the fruit of thy womb Jesus—"

"Amen," a voice rose.

"Yes Lord," another black Protestant cried, injecting an unaccustomed emotionalism into the prayer. I spotted my mother and Thelma exchanging quick glances. I tried not to laugh when my mother turned and rolled her eyes at me.

"Holy Mary, mother of God, pray for us sinners—"

"Please Jesus, yes."

"—now, and at the hour of our death, Ah-men," the priest concluded.

"Amen," a voice echoed.

Aunt Glo stood in the kitchen of yet another apartment after the funeral. "It was nice of you to come all the way from Miami," she told me. "How come Kay-Kay wouldn't come?"

"She's angry," I said.

"Angry at what?" she snapped. "What has she got to be mad at me about?" I peered into my aunt's eyes and wondered what was behind them. "I don't know what I did wrong," she said. "Your mother is lucky, two fine kids. But my kids, I lose them to the streets."

Jeffrey's daughter, a beautiful girl of about eight, sat quietly in the living room. Her father was dead and her mother had last been seen shooting up in a hallway. Aunt Glo was going to raise her. I looked around the room. The furniture was old, worn and different from the solid pieces she'd had in previous apartments, but she still had her complete set of encyclopedias.

# Who's Bad?

I crossed my fingers and hoped by the time Jeff's daughter reached puberty she wouldn't be pregnant and lost to the streets, too.

When I returned to that apartment three years later, Jeffrey's youngest sister was in college and planning to become an attorney. His daughter was a very independent young lady of about eleven. We went shopping one afternoon and she spent the night with me at my mother's house. The next morning, she had already carefully made her bed and was fixing a bowl of cereal when I found her in the kitchen.

Aunt Glo asked me later how she'd behaved and I said great. "I told her how you could take care of yourself and run the house when you were just a little girl. She's got to do the same thing," said my aunt, her once-green hair now in a short, pretty, salt-and-pepper Afro, all her teeth gone, emphysema cutting her breath short. "She's got to know how to do for herself," my aunt said. "I won't always be here."

After her thirteenth birthday, almost to the day, I learned my hopes for Jeffrey's daughter were in vain. The street now owns her and she can be found on it at the midnight hour, with my aunt's consent. And my aunt, who still rarely has the energy to leave home, can work up enough steam to flail her arms and shriek profanity to anyone who tells her someone else should be raising Jeffrey's child.

# Aunt May

*I* don't celebrate Christmas. My father, a drunken Marxist, made that day of the year as much of a nightmare as all the rest. My mother is a fallen Catholic. I, never baptized, am a "heathen," as my aunt May used to declare. Nonetheless, I do believe in peace on earth, goodwill toward everyone, and I like old people.

Aunt May was old. It was her ninety-fourth Christmas, I think. To this day, I don't really know how old she was that year, 1977. No one knew her age. My grandmother, who was eighty then, always made a point of saying, "Your Aunt May was *already* a young lady—a grown, horseback woman—when I was *just* a little girl." They were half sisters.

Grandma and Aunt May didn't get along. Aunt May, you see, passed for white when she came to this country from Jamaica. She was tolerated in varying degrees by most of the family and despised by my grandmother. When the two were present for holiday gatherings, it was farcical.

"No!" my grandmother would bellow, stomping her foot or, as time passed, pounding her cane on the floor in protest. "I will not be seated with that woman." My mother would send me to the parlor to scout out the hostile territory. Was pressure building? Had blood been spilled? she wanted to know.

I usually found my grandmother Ruby Hyacinth Duncombe Lord seated in one corner of the room with her Chivas Regal–drinking church cronies brought in for moral support. In another corner sat my great-aunt, Marie Emily Pinchmant De Leon, and various family factions.

Grandma believed that Aunt May's crimes went beyond renunciation of race, including the "theft" of cash and property from their mother's estate that "rightfully" belonged to Ruby.

Who knows?

What everyone in the family does know is this: Aunt May came to America at the turn of the century and told white people, "I'm Romanian." A gypsy, I guess. She was a seamstress and the lie got her into the International Ladies Garment Workers Union, which didn't accept blacks back then. She had pale skin, finely chiseled features and long dark hair.

She'd married, but had no children. She seemed close to no one after her husband died except my mother, and consequently my brother and me. Because of this, my mother asked me to go up to her apartment in the Bronx that Christmas day. I was in graduate school at the time, living on Columbia University's campus.

It was not a bright, white Christmas. It was a gray New York winter afternoon when snow half melts, turns to slush, then freezes. A December day that leaves you in a knot from muscles tensed too long in the cold. I was tired and had to take the bus.

Aunt May lived in a housing project on Willis Avenue in the South Bronx. I had last seen her two years before, when her hair was still dyed jet black. The strands were a yellowed shade of white now. Bent by arthritis, grasping her metal walker, she struggled to the door to greet me.

"Darling, your Aunt May can barely see you," she said, her eyes milky with cataracts. She made it back to the living room and fell onto the sofa. It pained me to see her so helpless.

# Aunt May

I was fond of Aunt May, and I enjoyed the company of older people. But frankly, I would have preferred to spend the day with an old person I didn't know. My family is too large, too loving in ways that negate the love itself, and too demanding. Painful history and present tensions always combine when we meet. They drain me. I would prefer to love them from a distance.

From the living room couch, Aunt May tried to give instructions on lighting the stove and finding the plates. Finally, "You know what to do, dear," she said, her voice collapsing like a punctured lung. When she was younger, she spoke as a dramatic soprano sings, high but with power and resonance, the sound of the British Isles more evident in her Jamaican accent than most. Her voice and manner always evoked for me one of those matronly characters in a Dickens novel: five feet three inches of Victorian-like propriety.

"Whhaaaat!" I recall her reprimanding me years ago. "Young ladies do not whistle. A whistling woman and a crowing hen are an abomination to the Lord." I can see her thin lips parted in shock now. They parted just as easily to make way for a big meal and a tall drink.

"Yes, I'd love something cool to drink," she'd say at dinners my mother used to serve. I was a little girl then and amazed to watch her down a tall iced-tea glass filled with the Manischewitz Concord grape wine and ginger ale concoction my father loved. Three blinks and it was gone. And she ate like a vulture, a family trait. Like my mother, she'd pack away a meal for two, daintily dab her mouth and then sigh with satisfaction: "Just a little something to hold body and soul together." Hers were disintegrating now.

Her voice seemed to come from a tiny hole in the corner of the living room; it was still high but muffled, as if it was struggling to reach me through a wad of cotton batting.

We ate a turkey dinner my mother had prepared and left a few days earlier. *The Sound of Music* played on TV while the snow turned to slush and blackened ice on the grim South Bronx streets below. She lived on a block opposite the Catholic church she loved and surrounded by Borinquens she loathed. Except for the gypsy she passed as, Aunt May didn't seem to like too many races or nationalities.

Years earlier, sick in the hospital, Aunt May denied she was related to the obviously black relatives who came to visit her.

"Even at her husband's funeral," said my grandmother, "she ignored me. I came late, but there was a seat for Mrs. Lord. They called out my name and told me where to sit. But she told no one I was her sister. She said I was a friend."

But Aunt May's husband, Grandma said, "was such a nice man." Vernon De Leon.

He was a fair-skinned Jamaican, too. "He looked Latin," my mother says. "Olive complexion, straight black hair, sharp features. Most people would have thought he was Spanish or Italian. He was a lovable, down-to-earth drinker. He loved to go out with the boys every Friday night." Before he did, "Aunt May was waiting on the corner for him to get his paycheck."

Vernon De Leon has been dead most of my life, so I don't know what he told people he was. As for my grandmother and Aunt May, their family was African and English and French, East Indian, Chinese and who knows what else of what was thrown into Jamaica's New World culture. But Aunt May's father was a European named Pinchmant.

My grandmother, divorced and trying to raise four children in the midst of the Depression, got a visit from childless Aunt May. "She didn't know I was in the house," Grandma recalled, "but I heard her." "Oh, I'll take this one," said Aunt May, pointing to my grandmother's lily-white fourth child, Gloria.

"Never happen!" said Ruby Lord. "You want her because

she's light like you. You want one, you better want them all. But that'll be over my dead body."

Colorstruck as she was, Aunt May was particularly fond of my mother—definitely not the fairest of Ruby Lord's children.

"I was the only one who used to visit her," my mother said. "I don't know why. I always liked older people, and she was a relative. Now basically, there is no question she was prejudiced. There's no excuse for that. From what I gather though, times were very hard. People assumed she was white and if she could get away with passing, she just left it that way.

"But she was always nice to me, so there was no reason for me not to like her. She always gave me a little gift, too. I was a kid, maybe that's the reason I kept going back."

Aunt May was always kind to me, as well. She never failed to slip ten dollars in an envelope and mail it to me on birthdays and Christmas.

We talked very little after dinner, but I sat close to her and held her hand while we watched TV. When she began to sniffle and tears welled in her eyes, I thought it was because she was thankful for the company and touch of another human being. She was incontinent.

"I want to die," she cried, as I helped her up from the couch she had wet. "Oh God, please, just let me die."

I took her to the bathroom and tried to bathe her. She went limp on me. I was 105 pounds and she was about 160. I dragged her from the bathroom to the bedroom. Her limbs were dead weight as I lifted them to dress her. I stayed the night.

Nearly a year later she lay dying in a Bronx hospital. It was almost Christmas again, and when her family came this time, she did not deny us.

# No Fools, No Fun

M y aunt spoke through clenched teeth. "Willie . . . Willie . . . Willie!" she snapped finally.

Her beleaguered-sounding husband drawled a response, "Yesssss, Rae." He knew he better come. She used to keep a big stew pot filled with boiling water on the stove as a threat if he got out of line. The pot of hot water was gone, but all she had to do was raise an eyebrow, suck in her cheeks and intermittently tilt her head toward the kitchen while she did the I-dare-you-chicken move with her neck—back and forth, back and forth—and he knew he better step.

Willie was lean, handsome and seemed like such a nice, easy-going guy. Maybe that's why he drank. The constant threat of being in hot water was just too much for him. I don't know exactly what he did to deserve it. Maybe he was just taking the weight for the crimes of Aunt Rachel's previous husbands. He was always nice to me. When I visited my aunt as a kid, he waited on me hand and foot.

"Can I get you anything? Would you like this? Are you sure you don't want that?" He was a gracious North Carolinian, always the soul of hospitality. And as a child I saw him frequently. I stayed with him and Aunt Rae off and on during junior high school.

Their South Bronx neighborhood was closer to the school I was illegally attending, Castle Hill Junior High. I had lived in Harlem when I first went there, not too long a haul. But by the time I was in the eighth grade, I'd moved back to Brooklyn. My mother knew it was important to keep me in a good school, but that trek was too much, so I often stayed with my aunt.

She had a pleasant, three-bedroom apartment situated in the middle of a street that resembled bombed Beirut, just around the corner from the place where they filmed scenes for the movie *Fort Apache, The Bronx.*

As for Aunt Rachel and me, we got along fine. I'd lived with her before, when I was about five. She was living in Boston and was married to a guy named Pop then. My mother, while she worked as a registered nurse, was having a difficult time finding child care. My grandmother, who usually took care of me, had gone to Boston to live with Aunt Rae. So I went there, too, joining several other cousins who'd arrived ahead of me.

Aunt Rae's daughter Karen and I were the only black kids in the Prince School in Boston on Exeter Street. And I was in that school illegally, too—too young. Aunt Rae altered my birth certificate to get me in. I could read before I was four so she saw no point in keeping me out of school. She skipped kindergarten altogether and put me in the first grade when I was just shy of five.

It might have worked if the school nurse, originally from New York, hadn't spilled the beans. She'd worked with the doctor who had given me my smallpox vaccination—three times. The first two attempts on my arm didn't take so I was finally vaccinated on my thigh. She remembered. "I know this child," she squealed.

I got kicked out.

Aunt Rae put me in another school. They found out. I got kicked out again—twice before the age of six.

# No Fools, No Fun

Aunt Rae wasn't supposed to have any kids in her Boston apartment on Albemarle Street, just a few blocks from Symphony Hall. When the landlady visited the building, I had to hide under the bed with my other cousins. I thought that was great fun, very dramatic, a chance to pretend.

I don't think the landlady knew my aunt was black. I don't think she would have rented to her if she knew. She knew we weren't white, but like the people on the block of every Back Bay apartment my aunt rented—three of them—she thought we were Portuguese or Cape Verdians. I guess these people weren't used to seeing such extreme color variations in one "black" family. One cousin looked like the Beaver, Karen looked like a Senegalese princess and the rest of us were olive-skinned and cinnamon-colored and what my Guyanese relatives call a sapodilla brown. Hardly unique, but white Bostonians in the 1950s couldn't get a handle on it. Or maybe they did finally figure it out, and that's why my aunt moved three times in a very few years.

In Boston, Aunt Rae taught me mass transit survival techniques. "Okay, baby," she'd say, "when you get on the subway and it's packed and the crowd won't let you through, elbow." She'd fan her arms so that her elbows pumped out. And then she showed me how to put my shoulder in it if the crowd wouldn't give an inch or pressed back.

Aunt Rae felt I had the right stuff to do it, even at five. She liked me a lot and I looked a lot like her. We wouldn't scare anybody, but we weren't beauties, like my mother and Karen, who people said seemed more like mother and daughter. Aunt Rae and I were as mischievous and extroverted as they were prim and reserved. She wanted to be in show business, a dancer I think. And she knew I wanted to be a singer more than anything in the world. I told her so when I was barely four. That's when she first met me.

I opened my mother's apartment door and Aunt Rae was face-to-face with space. She had to look down to see me. "Hello, please come in," I greeted, with barely a tooth in my head—I was precocious in everything but acquiring teeth. "May I offer you a drink?" That's what she told me I said. It was an ominous greeting.

When I look at pictures of her—with uncles, cousins, friends, me—a bottle is always present, a glass is always full. I should have recognized what was happening to her. Like my father, an alcoholic who drank from Mott's applesauce jars, the ritual end to her evenings came when she placed wax paper over her unfinished cocktail, then secured it with a rubber band, or poured it into an empty peanut butter jar and screwed tight the lid.

It was the Fourth of July, Louis Armstrong's birthday, and tar was bubbling between the cracks in the city pavement. It had been one of the hottest summers on record in New York. Aunt Rae had decided to forgo her usual urban summer holiday barbecue on a rooftop or under a bridge, preferably the George Washington, and journey to the sticks—Brooklyn. My mother was holding a big family cookout in the backyard.

Aunt Rae would have made a great professional cook, despite her hoofing ambitions or family expectations that she'd be an attorney because she was so smart and combative. She made a mean, mustard-based barbecue sauce, jars of which were ready to be transported to my mother's.

We rose early that holiday morning and began carrying the sauce, ribs, chicken, potato salad and six-packs of Champale to the first floor. It was four steep flights from the apartment to the narrow, ground-floor hallway where we waited for the car.

Despite her mastery of mass transit survival techniques, Aunt Rae avoided the subway whenever she could. No matter how great the distance from borough to borough, she preferred the often circuitous route of buses to being underground. But Flatbush was too far from the South Bronx, the day too sweltering and the load too heavy for the bus. She arranged for us to go by car.

Willie, Aunt Rae, Karen and several other cousins stood in the tight tenement hallway waiting. When the car came, one of us was to get my grandmother, who never let a week go by without reminding us of the flotilla of servants she'd had in Jamaica—much to Aunt Rae's annoyance: "Mama, no body wants to hear that. That's why people don't like you West Indians, always bragging about what you had before you got here." Of course, the cultural subtext for my aunt's proclaimed disgust was African-American resentment of West Indian high-handedness. And she, like the children of most immigrants, wanted to be accepted by her peers, most of whom were African-Americans.

I stepped from the hallway to the cracked front stoop to see if the car was coming. It was early in the morning and blindingly bright. In the middle of the block, a vast, junk-heaped lot held tons of smashed glass and crushed aluminum cans that reflected the powerful sunlight, making them glitter like precious things they were not. It resembled the poverty of the tropics, where the unrelenting sun sears the ugliness into your eyes.

A car turned slowly into our block, rolling past all the other walk-ups before ours. Willie got Grandma.

The chauffeur got out of the long, black limousine and tipped his hat to my seventy-year-old grandmother, who was smiling girlishly. "Madam," he said, "my name is Clarence." He helped her into the limo, where she sat in the front next to him. My cousins and I, Willie and my privilege-eschewing aunt piled into the back.

With the raw ribs and chicken, potato salad, Champale and

barbecue sauce loaded in the trunk, we rolled across the potholed street with barely a bounce, passing the glitter in the junk-heaped lot.

When my mother saw us roll to her door and unload the rattling jars of barbecue sauce, she shook her head and muttered, "No fools, no fun."

Several years after that Fourth of July, Aunt Rae and Willie moved into a big co-op apartment she'd purchased in Harlem. It had a long terrace she never used—perhaps because it over-looked the Seventh Avenue IRT subway terminal—and she still preferred barbecues under the shade of the George Washington Bridge. The walls of the spacious apartment were made for art, which she never hung. She liked a blank, white wall, she said. When I visited, the end table next to the living room sofa always held a pack of cigarettes and a cocktail in a jar.

Growing up, I never saw her drunk. Willie, on the other hand, blacked out regularly. He had been taken to Harlem Hospital so often we never expected him to return.

By the time I was in my twenties, I'd find him sitting in a living room chair nodding, while my aunt sat on the sofa drinking, smoking, staring at the TV. She talked to me when I visited, but her eyes were almost always focused elsewhere.

After several decades, she'd lost her job as an accounting clerk when her employer went bankrupt. My aunt had no other skills. And she was totally intimidated by the process of job hunting, and humiliated by the rejection she received when, nearing sixty, she tried.

My grandmother was living with her, too.

"I don't want it," Grandma said, refusing to eat the plate of food Aunt Rae put in front of her. She threw the paper plate at my aunt, splattering the juice from the greens and the gravy from the roast on the freshly painted, white kitchen wall.

# No Fools, No Fun

My aunt picked up the plate, put the food back on it and planted it on my grandmother's head.

My grandmother, nearing ninety, got up and took a rag to the wall Aunt Rae was already scrubbing. "Did it get messed up badly?" Grandma asked softly, her dinner still dripping down her face.

"No, Mama, not bad," Aunt Rachel said, wiping the blotched walls.

I had been away from home for years and saw Aunt Rachel irregularly after college. But Karen would later tell me Grandma and my aunt had been "enmeshed in a fatal dance for years."

I was visiting Aunt Rae, not long after Grandma's dinner had decorated the wall. There was a commotion in my grandmother's bedroom. Her health was failing and she was complaining loudly of pain. Everyone in the house but Willie rushed to her room. When I stepped out, I found him in the living room walking around in circles, talking to himself: "Is there anything I can get you? Is there anything you need?"

I don't know who was driven to drink by whom first. The spouse who seems most passive is often the one most hostile and the trigger for the other person's more obviously belligerent behavior.

In the fall of 1987, my aunt was seventy pounds and near death. Karen decided on a family intervention to get her into an alcohol treatment program. But she became so sick she had to be rushed to the hospital before it could be done.

Shortly before her release, my cousin, my brother and I—with the help of a counselor and doctor—tried to convince her to enter a treatment program. She refused. We knew she couldn't take care of herself. But it was apparent that she'd have to bottom out before anything else could be done—if there was still time to do anything.

Several days after her release, my aunt had to go to the hospital for a follow-up appointment. I called her to make sure she was going.

For the first time, she admitted how frightened she was, how confused. I told her I'd take her to the hospital, and I decided I'd try one more time to get her in a treatment program.

I got her out of the house and into a cab. Willie tried to get in the taxi with us. He had been giving her liquor since she got home, happy to know, I think, that they were in the same sinking ship.

"That's all right," I told him. "I'll take care of her."

"He's got my money, my credit cards," Aunt Rae said.

"Give them to me," I told him. He tried to get in anyway. "Uncle Willie," I said calmly, "I need you to stay at the house and hold down the fort."

He shrugged. "Okay," he said.

There was nothing for him to take care of but himself. My grandmother had been put in a nursing home.

My aunt was frail and barely able to walk. The hospital personnel kept directing us to the wrong place, and we spent an hour covering one square block, my aunt holding on to my arm, looking lost, disheveled and frightened. Had I passed her on the street, I'd have thought her a homeless bag lady.

When we finally got to the right place, the nurse asked her the day and the date. My aunt, shaken by tremors, had not forgotten the importance of charm to one without beauty. She gave the nurse an ingratiating smile. "Well," she said slowly, her eyes roaming, "I'm not sure about that."

"What year is it?" the nurse asked.

"Ah . . ." My aunt struggled, putting a trembling finger to her bottom lip. Then she answered with a careful smile, as if she were a game show contestant who didn't want to look foolish to millions on camera if she answered incorrectly. "1981?" That was seven years ago, the last time she worked.

# No Fools, No Fun

The nurse consulted with a doctor and they were ready to admit her to the in-hospital treatment program—the best in the city—immediately. But life isn't always like a made-for-TV movie. My aunt wasn't Betty Ford. She didn't have the necessary insurance. They wouldn't take her that day. She was put on a long waiting list while she tried to get the necessary medical coverage.

Seven months have passed, and she probably wouldn't go to the hospital now, anyway. She is drinking; the doctors say it will kill her—soon.

Willie blacks out more often than ever. Aunt Rae just leaves him on the floor, says my aunt Glo, who brings her food. He'll get up eventually, Aunt Rachel reasons, then just fall out again.

Another six months have passed. It is Christmas night and my mother is on the telephone. She is disturbingly calm. Aunt Glo's kids took Aunt Rae Christmas dinner. She grabbed it and began to eat voraciously. I hear my mother's heart in her throat as she tells me. The kids tried to get Willie to eat, but he wouldn't move from his chair when they called.

"Willie," said a cousin. "Willie . . . Uncle Willie. . . . Aunt Rae, he's cold, he's so cold. . . . He's dead."

"Yes," said Aunt Rae, lifting a fork full of food to her mouth, "I know."

# Bag Lady

*I* have locked my mother in the bathroom. I am in there with her. I am blocking the door and refusing to let her leave not just because she wanted me to transport twenty pounds of Carolina Rice from New York to Lakeland, Florida—where she now lives and can't get her favorite grain—on my way to Miami, where I live. Nor have I bolted the door simply because she now wants me to take a new, soft-sided weekender—just big enough to *not* fit under the seat of a plane or in a compartment above it—back to Miami for my brother who will visit me there soon. I haven't prevented her exit from the can merely for these things, despite the careful logistics of my own travel: carry-on luggage only, each piece weighted not to stress my increasingly bad back, also allowing me to bypass baggage claim, where suitcases are sure to be late or lost, and giving me a carefully timed hour and fifteen minutes to dash through the airport, get through expressway traffic and reach my office for an appointment in Miami.

That she would prefer to turn me into a personal cargo carrier, rather than put the bag in a box and mail it directly to my brother, is no reason to imprison one's mother. Besides, this is not unusual behavior for her.

No distance between points was ever too great, no occasion

too grand for my mother to dump a load of freight in my hands. "Jill," I recall her saying one Easter Sunday, as I stood dressed for the rotogravure—kelly green coat with an empire waist; black patent leather bag; high, black patent leather pumps; short white gloves and a white, high-domed, jockey-style hat Audrey Hepburn would have died for—"I want you to go up to 116th Street and drop this off for your grandmother, then take this to your aunt in the Bronx." Then she handed me a plain brown shopping bag and said, "Good-bye, enjoy yourself."

We lived in Flatbush and I had to ride several trains through several boroughs to make the demanded deliveries. I swore that when I grew up I'd never be dressed to kill and stuck with a plain brown shopping bag again.

My mother is yelling. "Let me out. Girl, if you don't let me out of here . . . move, move . . ." She moves right, I move right. She moves left, I move left. If she backs up, she'll fall into the tub, the bathroom is so small. "I mean it, let me, let me, let me." She is sputtering mad now, and my mother doesn't anger easily. When she does, she is rarely verbal about it.

"You just want to walk around and look cute with that dog-gone Gucci-Gucci bag you bought here," she fumes at me.

"It's not a Gucci bag," I reply. "It's a Mitsukoshi shopping bag I brought back from Japan." And if they'd had shopping bags as pretty as Mitsukoshi's when I was growing up—bands of yellow, blue, white, red, black and green on glossy paper with beautiful yellow handles—maybe we wouldn't have had so many arguments about my having to haul cargo over the years. But this is not about the bags, this is not about my life as the family freight hauler.

"No, you can't leave," I shout, trying to suppress a laugh, because our argument is over no laughing matter. But I tend to laugh when I'm angry. Just as I tend to giggle at funerals.

# Bag Lady

My mother doesn't laugh to conceal her feelings. She gets high blood pressure and ulcers.

*Thump, thump, thump.* That's the sound I heard on the ceiling in our Brooklyn house when I was younger and my mother was bedridden with an ulcer attack. *Thump*, she'd strike with her bedroom slipper again. Translation: "Some cream of pea soup, please."

Sometimes her heavy slippers seemed like Gregory Hines's dancing shoes, convulsed by an epileptic fit: *da-dat, da-dat, da dat-dat-dat-dat, da-dat . . . dat*, signaling one of us to pick up the phone. A simple *dat-dat, da-da* on the kitchen radiator meant "Come and eat."

Sometimes events would warrant a wild rhythmic variation on this theme. As when I was fifteen. *Dat . . . da-da-da-da-da-da-da-da-da dat, da-dat, da-dat . . . da-da . . . da dat*, and so on, meant: "Send that boy home. It's after midnight." Fearing that this had not quelled any suspected adolescent lust, Ma thought reinforcement necessary. A noisy flip-flopping of slippered feet came down the creaky stairs of our eighty-year-old brownstone. My mother, in her infamous slippers, marched past the living room, where my boyfriend and I sat, into the downstairs bathroom, flushed the toilet, banged down the toilet seat, high-stepped past the living room and lingered in the hall opposite us, where she switched the light on and off twice before stomping upstairs to her bedroom. I often wondered if my mother secretly wanted to be a signalman in the army. Anyway, romance was killed for the night, the boy left and my mother—master of nonverbal communication—triumphed again.

My mother's personality extended beyond her feet. She was a statuesque beauty of West Indian parentage who longed to live in a house like those in *Better Homes and Gardens*. She had, however, a proclivity for knickknacks everywhere, cluttering too small a room in our Brooklyn brownstone with enormous mahogany furniture, and forcibly integrating a two-and-one-half-by-four-foot portrait of a Spanish matador with modernistic mirror tiles and a wood-and-bronze plaque of Dr. Martin Luther King, Jr., in the same room.

It was a big house, however, giving my mother space to experiment, and she managed to create a few rooms of well-balanced elegance—at least we had no plastic slipcovers in the house.

She still has the house in Brooklyn but moved to Lakeland with my stepfather when they both retired. The size of their two-bedroom apartment frustrates her *Better Homes and Gardens* imagination. She has again stuffed the place with too much furniture that is too big. And in a fit of manic energy—"When things get tough, the tough move furniture, vacuum floors and decorate" is her motto—she has turned parts of the apartment into a surreal garden. She has hung floral poster art and planted butterfly replicas—butterfly knickknacks for the coffee table, magnetized ones for the refrigerator, and as you enter the apartment, a winged, three-dimensional, blue-hued, bulging-eyed creature about a foot square protruding from a wall. Its grotesque size must be the result of the same genetic engineering that created the two-inch-in-diameter blue glass grapes that sat in a bunch on my mother's Brooklyn dining table for years.

But I haven't incarcerated my mother for these lapses of taste.

My mother thinks she is a tightly held secret. She does not believe, for instance, in committing things to paper. And once one does, "you should never keep it," she once told me, explaining why she had no letters from the past. "Everything you need to remember, you will."

But my mother suffers from protectively self-induced amnesia. She cannot or will not connect the dots. Her failure to connect the dots is why I've locked her in, the reason her hot breath is in my face. We have rarely been this close since the womb. I would like to have been closer, but my mother is not a kisser, is not a hugger. I am supposed to know that she loves me because my teeth are straight and my legs aren't bowed.

"Look at that girl's legs," my mother once said, disgusted with the young woman's parents. "They should have had her legs straightened when she was a child."

My mother is a retired nurse. In her forty-year career she has been a bedside nurse, a public health nurse and a hospital administrator. She was very good at what she did, and no nurse looked better in uniform. I loved to go to work with her when she was a visiting nurse. When we walked down the street holding hands, it was obvious from all the turned heads that she was impressive in her sharply tailored blue uniform and field cap. At age five, I thought all the stares were simply because of the uniform, the great work it symbolized—and that my mother was pretty. I know now, she was stacked.

Patients were happy to see her; the women too. Some were invalids, others temporarily bedridden. I could see they really needed her. She was gentle, efficient and gave good injections: Eyes on an alcohol-swabbed section of buttock, she sized the target, then made a quick hit. Her lightning swiftness made it seem almost painless. I know, 'cause she gave me plenty.

I didn't realize until I was grown that she cast a clinical eye on everyone. Of one boyfriend she said: "Very handsome . . . has a slight scoliosis." On my last trip to Lakeland, she looked down at my feet. "You're getting a bunion," she observed.

"Is that a bunion?" I asked. "I thought my foot always curved out like that." She shook her head. She was intimately familiar with my feet, she said, and assured me my foot had not always been that way. Then wagging her finger, she warned me to stop wearing tight, pointed-toe shoes.

With such powers of observation, I wondered, why didn't

she comprehend that something was seriously amiss when at the age of sixteen I came to the dinner table nodding; landing, nose first, in my mashed potatoes.

When she asked what was wrong, I told her I was having a migraine attack. Then I went to my bedroom and slept for seventeen hours.

Such behavior was not normal for a healthy sixteen-year-old, she later admitted a friend warned. The friend asked her if I was taking drugs. My mother couldn't conceive of my doing such a thing.

I'd been popping Thorazine for weeks. I'd discovered it among the samples in the doctor's office where I worked after school. When I looked up the indications for the drug in the *Physicians' Desk Reference*, I knew the supertranquilizer was my kind of chemical. I was not interested in getting high. I wanted to feel nothing—ever.

Why I should have suffered this psychic implosion at sixteen instead of nine, ten or eleven can be attributed, I guess, to the exacerbating confusion of adolescence. I'd been ripe for it for years, but I was a very controlled child. My seventh-grade homeroom teacher had her suspicions, though: "I find so much maturity in a twelve-year-old extremely disconcerting," she wrote. My behavior was not unusual for the child of an alcoholic, I would learn.

As a teenager, I felt as though I was the only adult in the house. My father was out of control and abusing my mother. For reasons I have never fully fathomed, she endured it for years. Because my mother worked, I was responsible for my little brother most of the time. I had adult responsibilities, and I had to keep adult secrets.

"No, I have no idea why she's so upset," my mother told my junior high school guidance counselor. I had come into school one morning the week before sobbing convulsively. The

# *Bag Lady*

day I did, I told my counselor what had happened: My father had decided to settle an argument with my mother by raising a hot iron to her face. I'd always been paralyzed by his violence before. But not that morning.

"Don't you touch my mother," I screamed, running at him. I knocked him to the floor and told my mother to "run, run."

I didn't understand someone who didn't know to run.

My father lay on the floor in shock. I discovered years later that he told a judge that I attacked him. The judge didn't go for it. My father thought I'd gone crazy. He stared at me and chuckled meanly. When he got up, he went after my mother, banging on the bathroom door with the iron. I wanted to call the police. But I was afraid of what my father might do to me if I did.

I got my seven-year-old brother. "Peter, I'm going to dial the police. When they answer, you tell them your name and address and to come right away. Your father is trying to kill your mother." This, of course, was not funny. But you don't know my brother. He's an innocent, just like my mother. A man with a dry wit and an easygoing, live-and-let-live manner. That's just the kind of kid he was, too.

"Hello," he said into the phone, lackadaisical and wide-eyed, failing to grasp the urgency of the situation.

"Tell 'em where you live, tell 'em where you live," I whispered frantically, afraid my father would appear at any moment. I said the address and he repeated it into the phone. "And tell them to hurry."

"Hurry, my sister said."

My mother had locked herself in the bathroom and my father was still banging on the door when the police came. My brother let them in. My father was furious. He'd never been exposed before. "Did you call the police?" he demanded.

"No," I said.

"You're a liar, just like your mother."

My mother had to leave the house she bought, because my father wouldn't. I had to beg the police to stay until my mother could safely gather our things and get out. It was a little before six in the morning, and I remember her saying how grateful she was that the police had come before our neighbors were up.

My mother says she does not remember the conversation with my guidance counselor the week after I'd called the police. Nor does she remember a meeting, several years before that one, with my doctor. I was a sickly child but increasingly plagued by psychosomatic illnesses. "Is everything all right at home?" the doctor asked. My mother was silent. I was eleven, looked at her stone face and decided to be silent, too. On this visit to Lakeland, when I have not brought the Carolina Rice, she has repeated that she does not remember these meetings. That is why she's a captive in the powder room.

At sixteen, when I took my nose out of the mashed potatoes, I was walking into the walls at school because of the Thorazine. I attended the school that inspired the movie *Fame*, and had to perform in solo voice class that day. But I could not hold my head up to sing, and there was something wrong with my voice. Singing was the the focus of all my energy, it muffled all the dissonance in my life. But I thought I was losing it.

In the kitchen where my father raised the iron to my mother's face, I was alone and it was after midnight. She had gotten rid of him, finally filed for divorce. But the weight of all those years seemed to press against my throat. My head was on the kitchen table, the knife was near my heart.

*"What stopped you?" the doctor asked, years later.*

*"I tried to do it. I had the point of the knife against my bare chest. And then I thought what my death would mean. What would happen*

# Bag Lady

*if I never sang again? That's when I decided I couldn't, the loss to the world would be too great."* The doctor nodded slowly, as I said, *"I guess my ego was always strong. I was a fundamentally healthy child."*

*"Well,"* he said, *"it is unusual for a sixteen-year-old to have quite that strong a sense of their global importance."*

I put down the knife and called my cousin Karen. She had recently been released from the mental hospital. She would understand. She had a parent who was an alcoholic, too.

A few weeks later, I told my mother that I had no intention of being crazy like the rest of the family. I had found a therapist. I was willing to pay for it myself if she wouldn't.

She puffed up, then said nothing.

Ten years later, my father was gravely ill. I was twenty-six. I had not seen or talked to him for several years. My parents were divorced, but my mother had gone to check on him at his Jersey City apartment. She begged me to visit him.

My mother did not seem to grasp how I felt about my father. She would send birthday and Father's Day cards and gifts to him in my name. She would have my brother take gifts to him, which she bought.

On one of his birthdays, she made my brother deliver a fish dinner to him. My brother got verbally abused as a thank-you. He called me from a phone booth afterward to tell me about it. He was in tears.

I called my mother. "Your children are old enough to decide for themselves if they want to give their father presents or not. You finally divorced him. If we don't want to deal with him, stop trying to ram him down our throats."

That she loved my father was apparent. Something more than love, however, compelled my mother to keep us together when logic dictated she do otherwise. Perhaps it was her conventional notion of "The Family." She didn't get to live it with her own family, maybe that's why she wanted it so much for her children.

She says little about her own childhood. "Slept on a trunk . . ." she once let slip. It seems that happened during the Depression in Harlem. As the oldest, she was responsible for her brother and two sisters while Ruby worked.

"The lesser of two evils . . ." is how she described her decision to move south and live with her father and her stepmother. The weather was better for her poor health (she'd had rheumatic fever) and her father would pay for her college education—if she became a nurse. She wanted to be a social worker, but my granddaddy Lord brooked no opposition.

It's hard for me to believe sometimes that Granddaddy was often as unkind to my mother during her childhood as my father was to me during mine. Granddaddy refused to buy my mother a dress for her high school graduation, and only a last-minute gift from Aunt Rene, Ruby's cousin, saved the day. "It was a beautiful dress," my mother recalled once, her lower lip trembling. She caught herself and pressed her lips, then sat more stiffly in her chair. "It was handmade, all lace and white."

Sometimes, my mother told me without rancor, she had to sleep on the hard cot in Granddaddy's infirmary instead of the house.

In the past, I'd heard Aunt Rae say that my stepgrandmother Madelyn, just a few years older than my exceptionally pretty mother, was jealous of her. But my mother would never confirm this. She never had an unkind word to say about Madelyn, who she raised me to think of as a second grandmother. Nonetheless, life with her father and stepmother seems to have been a Cinderella replay.

I guess my father was supposed to be Prince Charming.

She had definite ideas about who the father of her children

# *Bag Lady*

should be, and my daddy seemed to fit: a brilliant scholar, witty, not bad to look at and "he could waltz fabulously. Your father was light on his feet," she told me. Her role in the marriage was to provide firm but enlightened guidance—something, she complained, her mother never did.

The happy-family plan might have worked if my father had just sat around and been brilliant and witty. My mother certainly tried to fulfill her role. She talked to her children, for instance. She didn't believe in spanking. That she actually did spank— no, beat—me once indicates the seriousness of my crime.

I was about five. My parents were separated and my father had come to visit. My grandmother was taking care of me while my mother was at work. Daddy had bought ice cream and asked me to go to the store to get some cones—the soft kind. He put a five-dollar bill in my hand and off I went. I couldn't find the soft cones at any of the supermarkets in the neighborhood, but I certainly tried. I was gone for two hours. Finally, I went to the candy store. Think of what you could buy with five dollars at a candy store during the Eisenhower years.

I returned home with two brown paper bags filled with toy watches, candy lipsticks, bubble gum, swizzle sticks, spearmint leaves and Juicy Fruit gum. My mother, dressed in her visiting nurse uniform, grabbed me as I sauntered over the apartment threshold. "Where have you been? Your father sent you to the store hours ago."

I cast a glance over my shoulder at my father. He had a look I'd see again, the one time I told him I loved him. I was sixteen. "You'd be different if I had raised you," was his response to my declaration. It was my first and last offer of affection. But when I was five, he simply had the look without the words.

As if to vindicate herself, my mother whipped me all the way to the candy store, where she told the owner: "You know I would never allow my child to come in here and buy all this junk. Take this and give her the money back." He did. Then she beat me the full three blocks back home.

As I sat in my little red rocking chair whimpering, I blamed it all on my father.

"Please," my mother begged twenty years later, "just go over to Jersey and see your father. Just check on him."

"Why don't you go?" I asked. Then she said my future stepfather thought it best she have nothing more to do with my father. I agreed with that, so I relented.

I rang his doorbell, but he was too weak to come to the door. The apartment manager was bowling. I waited two hours for his return. When I finally got in the apartment, my father was lying on the floor naked and bloated. When the ambulance attendants came, he refused to go to the hospital. He knew his name; he knew the date. He was considered mentally competent and could not be taken against his will.

My mother knew all this. She had tried to get him to the hospital the day before, I found out. I was furious that she had let me stumble onto such a scene.

With the help of my father's friend, a city councilman, I got a court order to have him hospitalized. It took two days. By then, my father was so ill he wanted to be taken away.

A student of his—a young man my father had convinced to stay in high school and tutored—called me. The young man was home from college visiting. He was already at the hospital when I arrived. "I'm so sorry, your father is dead," he said tearfully.

No, I told the nurse, I did not want to see his body.

Hours later, I walked into my mother's kitchen in Brooklyn. My brother was sitting at the table eating. "Daddy died today," I told him. He was seventeen at the time. He said nothing. A few minutes later he left the room. I never heard him speak of our father again.

# Bag Lady

My father wanted to be cremated in a plain pine box without ceremony. He was an atheist. His high school students—many of them Irish-American and Hispanic Catholics—didn't understand this. My mother, though a lapsed Catholic, couldn't accept it either.

"But those were his wishes," I told her, standing in my father's apartment, packing his belongings. As I boxed his vast collection of books, bills from the liquor store fell from the pages. My mother had dumped the funeral arrangements on me and now wanted to direct things. I looked at her disgustedly. "When I die, I certainly hope people carry out my wishes," which were quite explicit. I intended to be mummified and placed in a crypt.

My father was cremated but there was a funeral as my mother wished. "That was your husband," I told her. "Things went on between you that I will never know about. If that's what you want, we'll have a funeral."

Of course my father couldn't just die and leave us in peace. He fancied himself a legal expert after studying the subject at Harvard. He left a substantial amount of money and multiple wills, all of them ruled invalid by a court. I was his oldest living heir, but I had been disinherited. My brother, who had never done him any wrong I know of, had been too. Since my mother divorced him, she got nothing either. What he had was going to go to strangers. I went to court to straighten out his estate.

My attorney—a middle-aged Irish-American who took objection to my African name—didn't like me. My father's friend, the city councilman, had recommended him and assured me he was one of the best attorneys in town. I was sick, about to have major surgery, and didn't have the energy to look for another lawyer. He called me at home.

"Why," the lawyer demanded, "did your father disinherit you?" I was in bed, a television commercial had just ended and

*The Gong Show* was coming on. I'd never seen the show before.

"Because my father battered my mother, I hated him for it and he knew it. What else do you want to know?"

"What had you done that caused the rift between you?" the lawyer pressed. I stared at the receiver. I heard the Unknown Comic introduced. "Did you and Dr. Morgan—"

"My father's name was Moreland, not Morgan," I snapped, "and I've answered your question." I hung up and lay in bed facing the white wall. A chipped piece of plaster had been smoothed with spackling compound and painted over. I ran my fingers over the slightly raised surface, then began to pick at it. I remember hearing someone gonged . . . the room darkening . . . a squirrel on my windowsill . . . night. I was still picking at the wall when my cousin Karen, with whom I lived, called my mother.

She was sitting in the kitchen, still in her nurse's uniform, when I finally got out of bed. "Is there anything I can do for you?" she asked. She was seated at the kitchen table, her hands tightly clasped. "Is there anything you need?" Her eyes examined me. I said nothing.

Finally, she rose and walked toward me, held my shoulders, looked into my eyes. "Is there anything I can do?" We tumbled into the long silence, fell through the space of years when questions went unasked, when answers were forbidden. When I'd circled time and returned, I sought my voice. It came out husky, and my words were slowed by the burden of their indictment.

"Why . . . did you make me live with that man?" It was easy being angry with my father. The rage I felt toward my mother was rooted in a sense of betrayal. I would have protected her against anything and everything. Why had she not protected me?

"I did not know you felt so strongly," she said that night in the kitchen.

# Bag Lady

"I hated him," I said, my eyes fixing her.

"You never said anything," she told me lamely.

"I was a child," I said.

That she could finally bring herself to say that night, "I should have left sooner; we all suffered because I stayed with your father," was the best I could expect. And it might have sufficed if the denial hadn't become a permanent aspect of my mother's personality.

When I told her I still went to a therapist, years after that night in the kitchen, she'd purse her lips and say nothing. My cousin Karen is also in therapy, partly because of an alcoholic parent—my mother's sister. She is also involved with Al-Anon and ACOA, Adult Children of Alcoholics. When she tries to discuss these things with my mother, the response is: "Well, if that's what you need." Then my mother cuts her off impatiently.

My mother still does not say my father was an alcoholic. That's one reason she's still in the lavatory. And now her sister is dying of the disease. My mother is in deep pain over this, unable to do anything to save her sister's life. Except to tell my cousin Karen she should be guarding her mother and locking up the gin.

Because alcoholism has destroyed the lives of people she loved and affected her, my cousin and I have suggested that my mother attend meetings of Al-Anon, a support group for the family and loved ones of alcoholics, or talk to a therapist about her feelings.

But my mother is clearly with those Americans who think the weak, the inadequate seek psychological counseling. She would deny this, of course, and just say she doesn't need it.

But her nerves are bad. I'm sure she'd say that's because she has a writer as a daughter. I know in some ways she's happier than she's ever been. Marrying my stepfather, a kind and intelligent person, helped. But just below the surface, I sense a constant anxiety. Her ulcer is under control, but oh, that hypertension.

I have let her out of the jane. She has to finish Thanksgiving dinner. Old friends from New York, who now live near Lakeland, are coming to dinner. The man in the couple is a recovering alcoholic, deeply involved with Alcoholics Anonymous.

Over dessert, my mother mentions that she knows someone with a drinking problem. It is obvious she would like some advice, but doesn't want to get too specific. No one should know her sister has the disease.

I am grinding my teeth. I ask the man about the effects of alcoholism on the family of the drinker. My mother has switched channels. It's time to clear the table.

I know my mother is the product of a generation that did what it had to do without whining, without running to shrinks every time there was a problem. She's a do-it-by-your-bootstraps woman if there ever was one. "Cast down your buckets . . ." she still likes to say, quoting Booker T. Even though she is a nurse, the daughter of a medical doctor—or perhaps because of it—the psyche is still undiscovered territory for her; that, or just too frightening to explore.

Fortunately for our relationship, I can and do connect the dots.

In a past life, I once was told, I lived in feudal Japan. My brother in this life had been my father then. He was a scholar, and against tradition, taught me all he knew, more than most men then ever knew. When he died, I was forced to marry a cruel man who abused me. My husband then was my father in this lifetime. At night, an old nursemaid would secretly come to my room and put salve on the wounds my husband had inflicted. "Your mother in this life was that woman," the psychic claimed.

# Bag Lady

Hmmmmmmmm.

My mother still thinks I locked her in the bathroom because of the bag.

"I don't think I've ever been so mad," she recalled months after I freed her. She was watching me pack the suitcase my brother never got. I took it, so I kept it.

"And when I think of all the grief you gave me over that bag," she said smugly.

At times, I still entertain the ridiculous notion that one can alter the pattern of another human being's life, that after six decades, my mother will change. Then I come to my senses and only hope my children will have teeth as perfect and legs as straight as mine.

# Carry-Me-Long

*T*he summer Russia invaded Czechoslovakia, my brother turned nine. We lived in Flatbush then, on a street of undistinguished brownstones and tenements on which a bus line ran. While the block lacked the architectural significance and peaceful seclusion of our old Clinton Hill neighborhood, it was ethnically more diverse.

To the right of us lived a Chinese-American family, planted between one from the West Indies and another from the southern United States. To the left of us was an Orthodox Jewish synagogue—the rabbi's shofar informing me of Rosh Hashanah and Yom Kippur. Next to it stood the home of newly arrived Haitian immigrants.

I don't know how much the cultural diversity of that neighborhood shaped my brother's perceptions, expanded his powers of empathy, but that August of 1968, when Dubcek's "socialism with a human face" was crushed by Russia, he sat down and wrote a story imagining what a Czech boy his age must have felt when he awakened and found tanks in the street, saw his country under siege.

When I was nine, West Indians and Afro-Americans defined my world. And though I had read everything from *Gray's Anatomy* to *War and Peace* at that age—I read everything I found in the house whether I understood it or not—I doubt that I could have then comprehended so intimately the suffering of people far away and unconnected to me. I had recently entered high school when the invasion occurred and still didn't give it much attention. So I was surprised to discover the story my brother had written—words carefully printed with pencil on several sheets of looseleaf paper—lying on the coffee table.

No teacher had asked him to do it, he told me. He did it because he wanted to. And that's all he said.

My brother didn't talk a lot. But he wasn't shy or an introvert. On the contrary, he was quite a showman.

*"Well,"* he growled, in a perfect Louis Armstrong imitation, *"hello Dolly, well, hello Dolly. It's so nice to have you back where you belong."* He dabbed his forehead with a handkerchief—my mother always dressed him in a suit with a handkerchief in the breast pocket. *". . . You're still goin', you're still glowin', you're still goin' strong."* He was five years old then and performing in the examining room of a city health department clinic. I had brought him in for some childhood inoculation, left him alone with the nurse, and fifteen minutes later, he was giving a floor show to the entire clinic staff. I mean, what could they have asked him in so short a time to have sparked all that? His name, maybe? The song ended but he wasn't through.

"And that, ladies and gentlemen"—he was Ed Sullivan now— "was the great, *rrrr-really* great, Louis 'Satchmo' Armstrong."

The kid was not inhibited. But he was a perpetual slow-motion machine in most things. He liked to nap a lot, and when he got up, he liked to take it easy.

"Carry-me-long, pick up your feet and get over here," my exasperated grandmother would say to him. But this boy was no fool. Why rush to take out the garbage, do the dishes, go to the store, brush his teeth, comb his hair, take a bath, or do any one of a hundred things my grandmother, mother or I were always ordering him to do?

He had no time for the mundane preoccupations of the bossy women in his household. He had far more important worlds to attend to: the psyche of a young boy under siege in Prague, a new variety act to perfect. Maybe his out-of-this-world demeanor was triggered by traumas suffered while he was still in the womb. He looked ancient at birth and his back was blue and green.

My mother had fallen so many times while she was pregnant with him, his entire back bore a bruise that lasted the first few years of his life.

His conception was not planned. My mother could not have wanted another child given her disastrous marriage to my father. I think her tumble down subway stairs and missteps off curbs were no accident. But once he was born, once he grew into a singing, daydreaming reality whose big, brown liquid eyes made strangers stop on the street ("What a handsome little boy . . . he's goin' be a lady-killer . . ."), she smothered him with love. He was not spoiled—he got spanked. (And it takes more than a misdemeanor for my mother to raise her hand. Actually, she raised a broom and went after him.) He was made, unwillingly, to cook and clean. But he was overprotected.

My mother wanted to raise a nice, safe (that is, acceptable) Negro boy in a country where no amount of acculturation was going to guarantee safety or success for a black man or woman. And she was intent on doing so at precisely the historical moment when the integrationist mentality of the Civil Rights Movement was being challenged by black nationalism, revolutionary rhetoric and urban rebellion.

The social battlefield of the late 1960s, veterans recall, was marked by frequent household skirmishes over: hair. "Don't cut it anymore," I pleaded as my brother cried and my mother—a moonlighting barber who always cut my father's hair, too—scalped him. She didn't like Afros that summer of '68 and her opinion hasn't changed two decades later.

Years before, I'd seen my father slap some green goop called Helene's Hair-Setting Gel on my brother's hair, beat his naps down with a brush, then put a stocking cap on his head. Even after all that, when it came time to remove the stocking cap, he took the brush—a weapon in my eyes—to his head again and futilely tried to bludgeon the kink out of his hair. When I saw my brother's agonized face, I turned away and went to my room to cry.

This time, as I watched my mother's metal clipper eat its way across his scalp, I threatened to leave home. I did leave home—for a night—distraught as I walked the streets of Brooklyn, despairing for a race that had been taught to hate itself down to the hair follicle. When I reached a girl friend's home, we shared our adolescent wisdom on the future of Africans across the planet. And, we agreed, when the revolution came we might even have to off our parents.

To this day, I don't think my brother realizes how much I suffered on his behalf.

When he was thirteen, I'd come home from college and find that he was still allowed to sleep in my mother's bed. I informed her, "This is not healthy," and cited all the necessary psychological data to support my point. As usual, she ignored me.

When I suggested she let him be more independent—go away to camp, hang out more with guys—she smiled indulgently but said nothing.

But my mother was an eminently practical woman, and it was inevitable that she'd one day tell him, as the song says: "Get a job." Just a part-time job after school. Something that would teach responsibility, provide discipline.

# Carry-Me-Long

"How about bagging groceries at the supermarket?" my mother suggested. He looked at her like she'd lost her mind, she told me later.

By the time I'd gotten my undergraduate degree, it was almost time for him to go to college, and he still hadn't held a job. So I called a friend who owned a jewelry store in Greenwich Village. Perhaps he could give my brother a job for the summer as a salesman, gofer, any kind of helper. The shop was lovely, in a great neighborhood, and the only thing he'd have to bag here was made of precious metals.

"Well, your brother is not exactly a go-getter," my friend told me after several weeks. He had to be pushed to do anything, and most of the time he just sat in the shop and stared.

I began to worry about my brother. We'd been close as children but lost touch with each other while I was in college. I did not know how to read his moods, which were marked by long silences and unembellished responses. My grandmother just said, "Your brother's dry."

I feared he might be suffering from the effects of my parents' violent marriage. My mother had divorced my father when he was relatively young, sparing him the worst of their brutal liaison. But he was so silent about his feelings I didn't know what damage had been done. A decade passed after our father's death before my brother spoke of him; and that was at my prompting.

"What can I say about Daddy," he responded flatly. "He seemed like a very unhappy man. I hardly knew him."

My life was more directly influenced by my parents' marriage, and it has resonated in every corner of my life. I could not believe my brother was left unscathed; he witnessed little, but enough.

The first time my mother decided to leave my father, it was because of something my brother said. I had just entered junior high school and had already left for class.

"Your brother heard your father yelling and came to me," my mother recounted years after the fact.

"Mommy, Daddy's not going to start acting funny again, is he?" my brother asked.

My mother said it hit her then that she couldn't let another one of her children live through this domestic nightmare. I was twelve and Peter was five. Why, I asked her twenty years later, had she waited so long?

She said she didn't know how she could have gotten herself into such a mess. She didn't know how she could have married such a man. And once she had, she was ashamed of her predicament and emotionally paralyzed.

And then I wanted to know, "Why Peter?" Why had the pain in his eyes made her move and not mine? I knew it was simply the moment; he spoke when she was ready to act.

But I also knew she had been protective of my brother in ways she'd never been of me. It seemed as if I'd always been expected to be an adult.

"I guess," she said one day, fumbling for words, "I felt a girl had to be independent, had to have a good education and be able to support herself. I never wanted my daughter to be weak and vulnerable—like my own mother was. And since you were naturally independent and capable, I encouraged that."

"You don't think a man has to be independent and capable?" I asked.

She nodded but didn't speak.

"Don't you know how to butter a piece of bread? Why do you have your elbows on the table? Are you sure you're related to me?" I was mortified watching my twenty-year-old brother eat in the restaurant of the National Gallery of Art with my mother and me. His knife was askew on the bread-and-butter plate, the crumbs from the roll he had tried to butter whole covered the white tablecloth. And his hair looked like it hadn't been brushed in years. Where was Daddy when we needed him?

"No, that's right, I don't know anything about etiquette," he fumed. "Who made up etiquette anyway? I can eat my bread any way I want," he said, snatching the roll off the plate and knocking his water glass over in the process.

"It's one thing to know the rules and break them as a matter of principle. It's quite another to just be ignorant," I said evenly.

My brother's retort was to stretch out his long legs—he was six feet four inches now—lean back, drape his arms across the back of his chair and glare at me.

"You better put those arms down before you pollute the place. We been tellin' you to get a stronger deodorant for years," I dug in.

He was a junior at Howard University and a slob. He was also . . . no, I can't say the word. Let's go back.

All the time we were trying to make him get a job, this slow-moving dreamer was absorbing the music of the universe. I was the one everyone expected to be a great musician. But without a lesson, my brother sat down at the piano one day and started playing. I think he was eleven. And then he started composing. Still, no one took this very seriously. Except for the poet and playwright Amiri Baraka. The summer I took my brother to live with me and other members of the Congress of African People, which Baraka headed, he gave him the name Sanifu. It means "composer" in Swahili. But it still didn't register with the family.

"Sneefu, come here," my grandmother would call.

"No, Grandma," I'd say. "It's Sanifu. Sanifu."

My grandmother had lots of grandchildren and she had a hard enough time as it was remembering his old name, Peter. But she tried. "Seefu. I mean Peter. No, now let me get this. What is this child's name?"

"Sanifu," I'd repeat.

"That's right, I'm sorry," she'd say. "Snafu, come here."

And when he sang and asked what I thought, I said, "Michael Jackson has a better voice." He was twelve, about the same age as Jackson, and looked at me with silent fury. Then he turned his back and continued composing.

Instead of going to a school for the arts as I did, he went to Peter Stuyvesant High, a school for students gifted in math and science. I think we thought he was going to be an architect.

By the time he was ready to go to college, he could play piano and bass *and*, I finally told him, carry a decent tune. He majored in music composition at Howard University and studied at the Berklee College of Music in Boston during part of his undergraduate education.

But he still hadn't held a job by the time he graduated. And from the looks of things, the women in his family complained, he didn't intend to. He stayed in the house composing and singing most of the time.

The only job I wanted him to get was in music, so he'd have some practical experience in the field. My mother hoped he might still become an architect or a lawyer. But I realized he was an artist, and as complete a musician as I'd ever met. I knew he could make a living. He didn't need "something to fall back on" outside of music, words that had been beaten into my head by my mother.

She never discouraged my interest in music, just my desire to be a professional musician. She pounded in the financial uncertainties of the performing life, the unsavoriness of the people who lived it. She thought every black woman in music was destined to live the life of Billie Holiday. I was always plagued by indecision when I had a choice between a nine-to-five job and a good but short-term gig as a singer. I wanted my brother to be psychologically free of all that. And I knew he had the talent to succeed if he were.

Twenty summers have passed since the Russians invaded Czechoslovakia; we are now in the era of *glasnost* and *perestroika*, and my brother finally has a job.

I am back in Brooklyn visiting. I am washing dishes and plugged into my Walkman, rocking to my brother's music. The enigmatic slob has become a romantic bard:

> *Yeah, somebody loves you that's right*
> *And maybe for her you could shed a little love light*
> *She won't mind if it's a whisper*
> *I know that her heart can hear you*
> *The fire and rain*
> *The passion and pain you feel*
>
> *I just got to know you'll . . .*
> *Stand . . . and deliver*
> *Give me that heart*
> *Baby stand, and deliver that heart to me . . .*
>
> *Yeah, somebody told me last spring*
> *He couldn't give the world, but he promised me one thing*
> *He said, I'm going to be the reason*
> *For love that you can believe in*
> *I'm here through it all*
> *Heart to the wall you'll see . . .*

Some critics say my brother's group, the Stand—composed of V. Jeffrey Smith, Sandra St. Victor and Peter Lord (AKA Snafu and Carry-me-long) is one of the most promising of the nineties, as evidenced by their first album for Atlantic Records, *Chapters*. A sophisticated blend of rhythm and blues, pop and jazz, the album had music industry insiders buzzing after its release. Now that I live in L.A. and run into entertainment industry types all the time, I hear strangers talking about my brother and his group: "The Stand . . . they're hot," commented a record producer who was in the same manicure parlor as I one evening.

But his work may be too sophisticated for the commercial sensibilities that *dominate* the record industry. Atlantic spent a great deal of money producing his group—especially for a debut album. But the company did little to promote them when, apparently, it became a choice of spending the limited resources allotted their black music division on a surefire commercial group or a more innovative one such as the Stand.

The black music divisions of record companies are not known for innovation. But Carry-me-long is signed to do several more albums for Atlantic and is successfully composing for and producing other artists.

I doubt, however, that being a success behind the scenes will be enough for him. It wouldn't be enough for me if I had his . . .

"Genius?" he yells at me one day, demanding that I say the word I've long refused to say. We both laugh.

"I'm your biggest fan. Isn't it obvious I recognize your potential genius status?"

"No. I want that explicitly stated," he tells me.

Right.

Not only is he more talented than I. I think he is more forgiving, too. I believe he wills himself to leave in the past any emotional baggage that could weigh him down. He is wise, in that regard. And, I have found, one of the kindest men I may ever know.

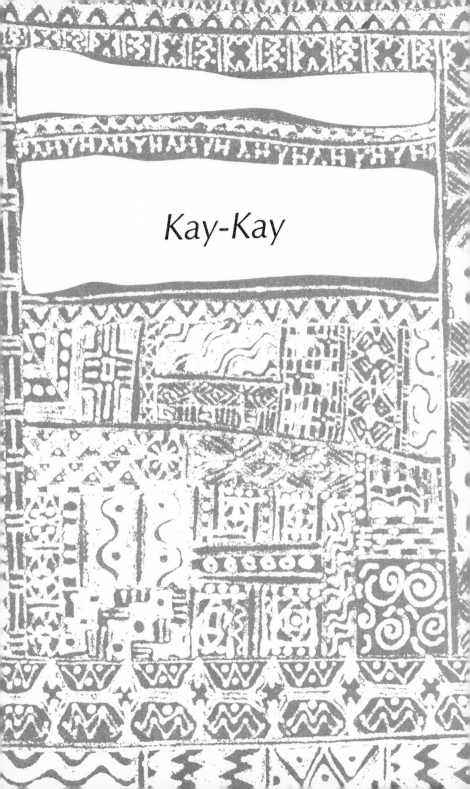

# Kay-Kay

E verybody loved Kay-Kay. She was our oldest and favorite cousin. But Kay-Kay loved me best.

I knew everything Kay-Kay knew, even though when I was five she was fourteen.

" *'Give us a song,' the soldiers cried, the outer trenches guarding—*"

"I know the rest," I said, interrupting her. *"I must go down to the sea again, to the lonely sea and the sky . . ."*

"No, cudaface, you Linkatara head," she said, and bopped me on the head with her poetry book. I loved it when Kay-Kay called me names. "That's 'Sea Fever.' "

"I know," I said. *"And all I ask is a tall ship and a star to steer her by."*

"Pretty good. You're gonna be something when your body catches up with your brains. Who wrote it?"

"The poet laureate," I answered.

"Which one?"

"Jayne Mansfield," I told her.

"No, you simpleton. John Masefield."

I was always getting things that sounded alike mixed up. Kay-Kay, who drilled me on composers and their music, once played Handel's *Messiah* on the phonograph and asked me to name it. " 'They Call the Wind Maria,' " I said. Well, they pronounce it Ma-rye-ah. Messiah. I also thought "Smoke Gets in Your Eyes" was "Salmon Croquettes in Your Eyes."

Kay-Kay lived with my parents, when they were together, even before I was born. Sometimes I lived with her and her mother and our grandmother and several other cousins. It depended on which sister was having a crisis at the time.

I liked it best when Kay-Kay lived with me, my mother and grandmother in our Brooklyn brownstone apartment. In the early evening, we'd sit in the living room reading out loud to each other while my grandmother cooked and we waited for my mother to come home from the hospital.

Kay-Kay got up to set the table for dinner. She laid a white place mat on the gleaming mahogany table that stood in front of the tall parlor window. Between the parted curtains, she spotted my mother stepping swiftly up the street.

"It's Aunt Vivien," she announced, "and she's moving fast."

"Hi-yai-yai-yai-yai," my mother greeted, entering the door. She inched her way into the apartment, turned left down the short hall and slinked—legs crossed, hands extended for balance—past the bedroom on the way to the toilet. I'd already raised the seat. She made it.

"What a relief," she said smiling, and plopped on the sofa, her legs stretched out. "How are you children?"

"What an embarrassment," my grandmother said. "A grown, horseback woman about to pee on herself. What kind of an example are you?"

"The word is 'urinate,' " my mother said brightly. "And I can't help it if weak bladders run in the family." She removed the bobby pins holding her nurse's cap in place, then rested the starched, winged thing on her lap. "What's for dinner?"

My mother kept a chart in the bathroom that Kay-Kay and I had to mark daily. My mother wanted to make sure everyone was regular. Kay-Kay had a lot of unmarked boxes on her section of chart.

Even with my constant sore throats, colds and rheumatic fever, she was more sickly as a child than I. We were both thin, but she had the most fragile bones I'd ever seen supporting human flesh. Her neck was long and slender, her arms, too, and her fingers were so delicate they seemed in danger of breaking at the slightest touch. She was beautiful, as well: dark brown skin with a hint of red, large eyes the color and gleam of black coffee, high cheekbones and long, thick hair. I always felt so ugly beside her.

On Friday nights, when my mother worked the late shift at the hospital and my grandmother was away for the weekend, we were on our own. It was tuna fish salad, barbecue potato chips, pickled cucumbers and grape Kool-Aid for dinner—followed by the "Marge and Kathryn Show." We lived for Friday nights.

Marge and Kathryn were the stars of our own soap opera. This was the late 1950s, and we'd been raised on radio melodramas by our grandmother. I think Kay-Kay was Marge and I was Kathryn.

"Marge, do you think Adam will ever love me again?"

"I doubt it seriously, Kathryn. You're such a hussy."

"But he must. Once he knows the truth, once he knows that I had to leave to save his life. I, I . . . Oh, Marge . . ."

"Oh shut up, Kathryn."

Kay-Kay said I was a ham even then.

By midnight Friday, the acid content in our dinner had taken its toll. Kay-Kay and I were covered with hives. My mother came home from work and found us asleep in bed, glowing in the dark: We'd dotted our entire brown bodies with pink calamine lotion.

When my mother moved from my first home in Brooklyn, Kay-Kay didn't live with us anymore. But we visited each other all the time. And she never stopped teaching me.

"I have found a gem of an aria for you," she said one day when I was fourteen. I had been studying piano for years and was preparing to audition for the High School of Music and Art, but as a voice major. I'd only taken piano because my mother made me: "A young lady should play an instrument," she said. She gave me two choices, the piano or the harp. Easy choice.

Kay-Kay placed the needle on the Leontyne Price recording. It was the Puccini aria from *La Rondine*, "Chi il bel sogno di Doretta," a favorite audition piece for sopranos today, but rarely performed twenty years ago.

Price possessed what my daddy called the "celestial vibration." It was never more evident, Kay-Kay and I thought, than on that recording. I had to learn that aria. But I had no private voice teacher at the time. I was, however, a member of one of the city's borough-wide choruses. It had a great director, Ronald Richard Smith—now an ethnomusicologist and a dean at the University of Indiana. I asked him to coach me.

He was reluctant at first. He wasn't a voice teacher, he argued, and he was justifiably concerned that I might damage my young voice singing so demanding an aria.

I begged for weeks.

He relented.

Six months later I stood beside a grand piano. The examiner asked what I was going to sing. I told her. She raised an eyebrow as I handed her the music. Before I had finished the aria, before I had even hit my high C, she stopped me. "That's enough." I believe I stopped breathing. She handed me the sheet music. "You're accepted," was all she said, without expression. I turned to leave, and through the window in the door saw that

# Kay-Kay

a small crowd had gathered. My future classmates applauded as I left the room.

"I was a hit," I told Kay-Kay.

"I knew you would be," she said.

As close as we were, there was so much we didn't know about each other's lives. It was twenty years before she knew the terror my alcoholic father caused in my life. And it was much longer before I knew how tortured her childhood had been.

When I went to college she claimed I deserted her, and really meant it. From that point on, we seemed to grow further apart. I was no longer the student and she the teacher. When I came home from college we shared an apartment for a while. She proved to be a monumental pain in the ass as a roommate. When she was unhappy, which was often, she wanted to unload morning, noon and night. When I was unhappy, I withdrew; I didn't want to talk to anybody. But if she had not been there when my father died, to help me sort out my contradictory feelings toward a man I thought I despised, my life at the time would have been much more difficult. In fact, no matter how great the physical distance, she has always been there to support me at crucial moments in my life.

When I started to write, she cast a critical eye on my work and declared I had potential. Then she gave me Zora Neale Hurston to read.

Kay-Kay should have been a teacher. It seems she has been everything else: lab technician, medical secretary, methadone maintenance counselor and most recently a day-care site inspector for the Department of Social Services in New York City. Not long ago, she was admitted to Columbia University, where she planned to get her master's in social work.

She was always a late bloomer, she says of herself. Acceptance to graduate school was a milestone in her life after marrying and divorcing one man, declaring herself gay and "marry-ing" an Italian-American woman—from whom she'd recently separated. I was there for neither the wedding nor the sep-aration. I remain ambivalent about her declared homosexual-ity—primarily, I think, because I believe she is really bisexual. Nonetheless, I've never done anything but defend her sexual orientation to the rest of the family. No, let me be specific, to my mother, whose attitude toward gays is: "If they just do it quietly . . . if they don't throw it in your face" they're tolerable. Since she loves my cousin deeply, she has managed to tolerate her homosexuality. I thank *Donahue* and *The Oprah Winfrey Show*, especially Oprah, for that. Things I've tried to convince my mother of for years she now gives credence because she heard them on or from Oprah.

But I don't think Karen's mother ever caught any of Oprah's shows on homosexuality. If she did, I don't think the talk per-meated her alcoholic daze. When Karen, my brother and I at-tempted an intervention to get Aunt Rae into an alcohol treatment program, the venom she directed toward Karen was perplexing to me. But I sensed it was related, in part, to Karen's homosexuality.

My cousin's relationship with her alcoholic mother has been as conflicted as mine was with my alcoholic father. But unlike me, she seems to have had little emotional stability in her early childhood. The first eight years of my life—the crucial formative period of childhood—were relatively idyllic, in great part be-cause of Kay-Kay's presence.

The trauma triggered by my aunt's sudden and rapid dete-rioration after years of drinking pushed Kay-Kay to the edge. She was hospitalized. I didn't know it for weeks, and she didn't call me when she got out.

"What do you mean not calling me," I yelled through tears over the phone. I accused her of trying to put me through a guilt trip because I'd "deserted" her years ago to go to college, then had left her to live all over the country when I became a journalist. I seldom had time to call. I rarely had time to visit. She was always sulking about it. And now I lived on the other side of the continent, Los Angeles.

"Don't you ever not call me again when you're thinking of killing yourself," I shouted. We both laughed.

She's not sulking so much anymore. I think she'll sulk even less when she finds out I have dedicated a book to her. Undoubtedly, it was through her love of literature, and her desire to share all that she loved with me, that I first learned the beauty of the word.

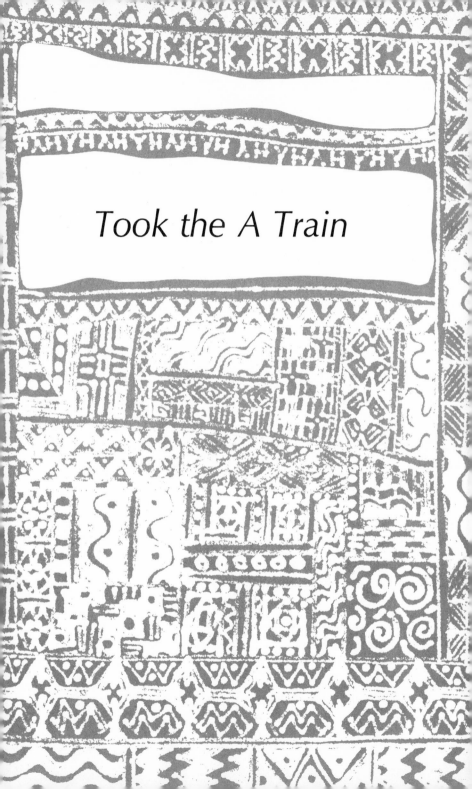

# Took the A Train

I was a mole. Aboveground, I could not find my way around New York City. Until I left the state, bought a car and drove back, I did not know I lived ten minutes from the Verrazano Bridge, or that Staten Island and New Jersey were practically in my backyard. I only knew the convoluted, subterranean routes of subways, and measured distance in time, not miles: ten minutes north to the Battery to catch the Staten Island Ferry; twenty minutes north to midtown to catch the PATH line to New Jersey.

My underground education began when I was almost eight and we moved from one end of the A train line in Brooklyn to the other end in Harlem. I had relatives to visit in both directions. My aunt Rachel had taught me how to elbow my way through rush-hour crowds. My seventh-grade teacher taught me how to fold a *New York Times* so it could be read, standing or seated, without bothering fellow straphangers—I believe this instruction is a mandatory part of New York's junior high school curriculum. But their instructions were insufficient preparation for life in the tunnel itself.

I was taking the quickest way to Harlem. A man sat in the single seat in front of me. I was in a two-seater next to the window, opposite the conductor's compartment and right next to the door that led to the other subway cars. The A train roared along the express tracks, the names of local stations whizzing past—Spring-Spring-Spring-Spring-Springininnnnnnnnnng... 23rd-23rd-23rd-23rd-23rd-233333333333rrrrrdddddrd . . . — with hypnotic incessancy.

I tried to blink my eyes faster than the flashing station names, then squeezed them tight and saw stars. The stars changed to toothpicks, the toothpicks stuck in the soap sculpture I'd done in Mrs. White's third-grade class a few weeks before. What, I wanted to know, happened to the end of the toothpick buried in the soap? What was going on down there? I was certain that wood and stone—all those things Mrs. White told me were inanimate—were jumping with life. But nobody else seemed to think so. "That's dumb," one kid told me. I tended to be talkative and outgoing, as long as I felt people were receptive to me. If I sensed that they weren't, I was silent and kept my thoughts to myself. I decided to keep my thoughts about the life of the toothpicks to myself.

The train pulled out of 34th Street and I felt something strange, something along the lower part of my leg. The man in the single seat was rubbing my leg with the back of his hand. I pulled back my legs, crossed them at the ankles, then pressed back into my seat. He never looked at me, just straight ahead. All I can remember now is that he was a white man with a sharp nose and a big Adam's apple. His arm dropped like dead weight to his side and his hand reached back for my leg. I squirmed and tried to shrink into the crack where the back of the seat met the window. I didn't know what else to do.

"Little girl." A black man in a hat, seated on the other side of the aisle, motioned to me with his finger as he called, "Come take my seat." I jumped up and took it. "What stop do you get off at?"

# Took the A Train

"One-twenty-fifth," I told him. He just nodded and said nothing else. I said nothing, too.

The train made the long, nonstop haul from 59th Street and Columbus Circle to 125th Street. "This is me," I told him, then jumped up and ran out the train door . . . ran along the platform . . . up the stairs . . . past the token seller with a bucket in his hand collecting the tokens in the turnstile. We spoke to each other all the time.

"Hey, where you flyin' off to?" he asked.

I did not answer. I just ran . . . and told no one why.

I was seated on the Pelham IRT train, in the last car, on the way to my junior high school in the Bronx. Two passengers in the car got off and I was left alone with a man on the two-seater diagonally opposite me. After several stops, the train lurched, throwing me forward. I saw the man and jerked back. He had his penis in his hand. I leaned back, my upper body hidden by the metal wall of the conductor's compartment. The train turned a curve on the elevated tracks, pulling me sideways. I saw the man again. He was ejaculating. I could not leave the subway car without passing him. I pushed farther back in my seat and heard a faint, rhythmic drip when the train stopped on the track between stations. His semen dripped into the puddle he'd already created. We came to the next station; I waited for the doors to open, then bolted.

I suffered many similar incidents between the pedophile on the A train and the exhibitionist on the Pelham-bound IRT. My subway experiences made me a hostile passenger.

"My mother has multiple sclerosis, I have diabetes and I'm blind in one eye. Please help the needy," the man's worn cardboard placard read. He was a handsome black guy who worked the Seventh Avenue IRT every weekday, maybe weekends, too. But I only saw him when I was traveling back and forth from my junior high school. He'd walk up and down the subway car thrusting his sign in people's faces, go back to the other end of the car, put down the sign and start singing. He had a great voice. Then he'd shake his tin cup in people's faces. I saw this man nearly every weekday for three years of my life.

Not long after the Pelham exhibitionist, the blind-in-one-eye singer jingled his tin cup in my face while I was trying to study for an exam. It had been a long day, almost two hours to and from school—Brooklyn to the Bronx—the train screeching along the tracks, the noise pollution wearing the nerves thin. My nerves were already frayed. I was thirteen and the week before I'd had to call the police to my house after jumping between my father, with a hot iron in his hand, and my mother's face.

The coins in the cup jingled. I ignored the beggar. He rattled the metal in my face again. "Lookahere, god damnit, your *mother* has multiple sclerosis, not you. And you're blind in one eye. Sammy Davis, Jr., is blind in one eye, too, and you sing better than he does. Get out of my face and go get a job."

Perhaps I was inappropriately harsh. Like the time I stabbed a boy named William, another fourth-grader, with a big rusty hat pin. All he said was, "You're pretty; I like you." By the fifth grade, unless I initiated it, I didn't want any boys bothering me. And tried to beat up the ones who did.

"You can't beat that boy up; he's bigger than you," Mrs. Johnson said, trying to pull me off some boy who had the audacity to grab me after school and kiss me. Mrs. Johnson was my fifth-grade music teacher. "You're just a little girl," she told me. "You can't fight him."

Eventually, I learned to be vigilant on the subways and on the streets. I didn't try to fight would-be molesters anymore, I just got out of the way if I saw trouble coming.

I saw trouble coming on the southbound Broadway IRT. I

was leaving the campus of Columbia University. I'd been away from New York for a few years and had lost my mole status. I was struggling to remember the best way to connect with the A train when a hairy man, weighing no less than 250 pounds, entered the subway car.

I was planted on one of those two-seaters again, next to the conductor's compartment. In a virtually empty subway car, he decided to sit next to me, squooshing my 105 pounds into the metal wall. His flabby arm—the size of two hams—pressed against me.

Despite my intermittent bravado, these thigh-rubbers still frightened me and the fear made me feel powerless. The best one can usually do is just get up. I started to. Then I changed my mind . . .

"Get up. You heard me, you slob. Get up," I shouted. The man looked at me incredulously, then moved to one of the long metal bench seats opposite me. He looked around the train at the other passengers, shrugged his shoulders, then threw his hands to the side, palms up, in a universal expression of confusion. Then he uttered something that sounded Greek—literally Greek.

I was undeterred. "Don't give me that 'I don't know what it's all about' garbage. You understand perfectly." I had an audience now, and the dozen or so passengers thought I was real funny shouting at a sheepish-looking Greek. But I stuck my nose in the air and looked straight at him.

I got up and stood at the door as the train pulled into the 59th Street station, the transfer point to the A train. I felt the eyes of the other passengers on me. The rush-hour throng covered the platform, waiting to stampede the train. The doors parted and I raised my left hand: "Hold it," I boomed. "Getting off." The startled crowd stood back, then parted to let me pass.

# Hair Piece

The king of curls in Opa-Locka, Florida, has no first name. He's just Mr. Vance. My hairdresser in Atlanta has no last name. He's just Kamal. In Miami, it's Raul. In New York, it's Mr. Joseph. This new breed of haute coiffeur was driving me mad.

"Hello, Mr. Vance, I'm a friend of Sujay's. I think she mentioned I'd be calling."

Silence.

"I'd like to make an appointment for a cold wave. Could you see me sometime next—"

"You'll have to come in for a consultation first," said a preoccupied voice.

"I see. Well, when can I have an appointment for a consultation?"

"I can do nothing until we consult."

"But you don't understand. I have a very busy schedule. If I have to take time off to get my hair done, I need to plan in advance, so—"

"You'll have to come in for a consultation."

The *b*'s in "bu-but" were exploding on my lips when he hung up.

"That's why I do my own hair," said Norma, standing over me laughing. There was a bald spot in the middle of her pageboy. "You had a call from the city manager's office while you were on the phone. And I have a doctor from the National Institute of Drug Abuse on hold for you now."

"Thanks. Let me call the city manager. Take a message from the NIDA guy, please."

I made the call, then walked to Norma's desk. On the way, I looked around the newsroom. I didn't see a single hairstyle that I liked on a black woman. Pageboys in 1981. Miami, what a backwater.

"What did the guy from NIDA want?"

"You can interview him the end of the week in Washington for your cocaine story."

"Great," I growled, one hand on my hip, the other trying to sculpt the hair at the back of my head into place.

"Your hair looks fine to me," Norma said. I was standing over her now. I had a direct view of the few wisps of hair covering a shiny, two-by-three-inch patch of scalp.

"I resent having to search from here to East Jablip for a competent hairdresser. You should, too. Don't you remember what black beauty salons were like twenty years ago?"

"No."

"How old are you?"

"Twenty-six," she said. "And you ain't much older."

"I'm trying to place this in some historical and cultural perspective for you."

"Really?" she said, her lips pursed, her eyebrows raised.

"Never mind," I said, and walked back to my desk. But I remembered.

They were where my grandmother bet a quarter every day on the numbers, sometimes more when she'd had a dream. "Here's a dollar, I dreamt seven-four-two last night. Play a combination." They were where *Let's Make a Deal* took on new meaning: hot goods peddled at record speeds to the music of police sirens. I once got a Borgana jacket, a pair of real leather gloves and a rabbit hat for twenty-five dollars. Had I been flush that day at Frankie's Harlem salon, I could have had a color TV and stereo for a hundred dollars.

But I liked my first beautician best. Her name was Mrs. Lane. She was our landlady, too, and ran a discreet salon on the ground floor of her Brooklyn row house. If hot goods were peddled there, it was done with the greatest subtlety. Or maybe my head was just in the shampoo bowl when they came. After my wash, Mrs. Lane would put me under the dryer, press my hair, then send me upstairs to our apartment for dinner. That gave her time to work on another head. When I heard a knock on the kitchen pipes, I'd go back down for a curl. I miss that.

"Mr. Vance? This is Itabari Njeri. I spoke to you a few weeks ago."

"Yes, I thought you would have been in by now."

"Well, it's my schedule. It's difficult for me to take time off for a consultation without some guarantee that you'll see me. At least give me an appointment that can be broken."

"As I explained to you, we can do nothing until we consult."

"If I come in for a consultation and you decide to do my hair, will you confer with my previous hairdresser?"

"That's not necessary."

"It's taken many trials and much error for hairdressers to find what works on my hair. My previous hairdresser knows all this. He can save us both a lot of grief."

"Then go back to your hairdresser if you like him so much."

"But he's in Atlanta."

"Then you have a problem."

I felt a migraine coming on.

Anne, the reporter next to me, leaned over the top of her video display terminal. "Itabari, why are you putting yourself through all these changes over a hairdresser?"

I looked at her freckled face and blond hair for a moment in silence. Then slowly I said, "Most white hairdressers don't know how to handle black hair unless they chemically straighten it first. I don't want my hair straightened. And a lot of black hairdressers, who use all sorts of chemicals for a variety of hairstyles, don't really know what they are doing. But the ones who do all seem to be a pain in the ass."

"Oh," she said, her head cocked like a dog's. I dropped it.

But even among the talented bastards, it was hard to know whom to trust. One stylist's concoctions left me almost bald, and I swore the next time that happened I'd sue.

But there was not going to be a next time, I told myself. Myself told me there was. I was having trouble sleeping at night. I began dreaming about baldness. There I was in a wig, on a date. My passionate companion clasped the back of my neck with his left hand and kissed me full on the mouth. The fingers of his right hand stroked my temple. And as he kissed me harder and pulled at my tongue with his teeth, his hand slipped under the wig's elastic band and his fingers became enmeshed in the netting.

Sujay swore by Mr. Vance. He had saved her troubled curls; maybe he could help me. After all, he had more than a salon. His business card said: "The Famous Mr. Vance's Professional Unisex Hair *Clinic* Salon. The hair clinic that embraces science, technology and you."

"How do you do, Mr. Vance. I'm Itabari Njeri. As you may recall, I'm the woman you gave such a hard way to go on the telephone yesterday."

"Oh," he said, surprised by the sight of me. I had dressed

for the occasion. I wore a sun-yellow tunic made of Indian cotton with matching jodhpur pants. The tunic was cinched at the waist by a cummerbund cut from the same cloth. The sash gathered the starched tunic's skirt and caused it to puff and stay like an air-filled shell. The wide sleeves billowed when I moved. Any moment, I could be airborne. I was a brilliant butterfly.

"Please have a seat," he said.

I patiently sat reading the signs in his small but attractive salon: NO CHECK, NO CREDIT, NO KIDS. THERE ARE TWO SIDES TO EVERY STORY. BUT I DON'T HAVE TIME TO HEAR YOURS.

This is the salon that embraces you?

"Now, tell me about some of the concerns you mentioned on the phone."

Butter wouldn't melt in his mouth. I relaxed, too.

I told him my troubles with past beauticians. "I'm determined to be more careful this time," I said.

"I feel sorry for you," he said. "You are a very unhappy woman. You don't trust people. No wonder your hair fell out."

"Look, I don't need a dime-store shrink. Are you trying to tell me it was my fault? It was the hairdresser's fault."

"That is speculation. We deal in facts here."

"Oh yeah? Well, when I went to the hairdresser, I had a full head of hair. A week later, my hair was in the sink."

"I wish you were as concerned about the other things I see wrong with you as you are about your hair," he said, staring at the enlarged pores on my nose and the pimple on my chin.

I wanted to deck him.

"Have you tried vitamins?" he asked.

"Look," I said, my voice spiraling toward hysteria, "I just worked a seventy-hour week at the paper, I can't find a decent apartment because people won't let me in the door once they see my black face, I got an editor who thinks that Jews and Italians are a separate race of people, and I can't get a bottle of my regular shampoo because the company doesn't ship as far south as Miami. You bet I look bad."

He smiled beatifically. "You are very attractive. You seem to be an intelligent woman. I want you to be satisfied."

He gave me a special shampoo and conditioner to use for a week before he did my hair.

"Mr. Vance, this is Itabari Njeri. That stuff you gave me left my hair bone dry and it's breaking."

"Yes. That'll be fine."

"What do you mean that'll be fine?"

"You must trust me. You have such a lovely voice."

"Thanks. But my hair is so dry it's breaking off."

"Yes, that's just the way I want it."

I wanted to cry. These pretentious shaft artists had forgotten their roots. Then I thought about Kamal. His shop was one of the few high-fashion salons that retained the warmth I remembered as a child. But he was in Atlanta.

I remembered Raul. A black woman had mentioned him to me before she left the paper and Miami. "In a pinch," she told me, "try Raul."

He was courtly and courteous. Unlike Mr. Vance, he consulted with Kamal by telephone and gave him his credentials. Things seemed to be going well. Raul handed me the phone.

"Don't let that man touch your hair," Kamal screamed. "I'm coming down there on the first thing smoking. He wants to put sodium hydroxide on your hair—lye. He wants to relax your hair, then put in a cold wave. You don't need that. Your hair will fall out again. I won't be responsible if you let anyone touch your hair. I'm coming down there this weekend to do it myself."

"That's not practical," I said. "It'll cost three hundred dollars just to fly you here and back and another sixty bucks to get my hair done. I can't afford that."

Besides, Kamal could mean trouble. The last time his fingers massaged my scalp it was a clandestine affair, carried out about midnight at the house of my girlfriend. He had just been sprung from jail for nonsupport of three kids and two ex-wives, one of whom he had married twice.

"No, Kamal, you'll have a horde of women thinking there's something going on between us."

"Noooooo, Itabareeeee, I'm straight now. I need a short trip to cool out anyway."

"Why do I feel you don't do this for everybody?" I told him I'd think about it.

I looked in the mirror. Nothing was wrong with my hair, I reasoned. I looked at *Essence*. I looked at the model on the cover. I looked in the mirror. I picked up the phone.

I called every kinky-headed, curly-haired Hispanic and African-American in the newsroom. I knew I wasn't the only woman who couldn't get the cut or curl she wanted from any hairdresser in town.

Within an hour, it was agreed. Five of us would fly him in and pay sixty dollars apiece.

Saturday night, nine-ten P.M., I went to pick up Kamal at the airport.

Nine-thirty P.M. No Kamal. How could I forget about old undependable? This is the man who would arrive three hours late for my appointment after I'd driven 144 miles from Greenville, South Carolina, to Atlanta just to have him do my hair.

Nine forty-five P.M. I call Atlanta.

"Itabareeeee, I'll be there. I tried to call you."

"You didn't try to call me, you jive so-and-so. 'Cause I've been home all afternoon, cleaning, cooking, preparing for you.

You've got two cold waves; one Afro cut; one wash, shape and trim and a potential permanent stirring restlessly in my living room."

"I'll be there, Itabari."

"Yeah, well you can call me from the airport when your feet touch Miami soil. Then I'll come and get you."

I went home and played my stress-reduction tape.

At eight-fifteen the next morning, the phone rang.

"I'm here." The voice was full of gravel.

"Who is this?"

"Kamal."

"I don't believe it."

"I told you you could count on me."

One of the other desperate heads, who lived close to the airport, went to get him while I whipped up the quiches and spiked the juices. The *Miami Herald* photographer arrived. My problem had become a sociological epic: the hairy plight of the black woman.

By day's end, our coifs were cover girl perfect.

Two months later we did it again; Kamal was two days late that time. During the fourth episode, Kamal called three days late to say he was "on his way." He didn't show. Not even vanity could compel me to maintain this shuttle beauty service. I called his Atlanta shop. I learned he was in a drug treatment program for cocaine addiction.

The long waits. The sudden disappearances from his salon. All Kamal's erratic behavior over the years became clear.

What was I going to do about my hair now?

A braider named Mashariki, who'd read the article about my search for a beautician, called me. She was considered one of the best African-hair sculptors in the country, she said. Perhaps I'd like to do a story about her, she said. I told her I'd be glad to stop by her salon one day.

# Hair Piece

"Have you read *Four Hundred Years Without a Comb?*" she asked the day I visited her shop.

"No. I'm not familiar with that one."

"Well, I thought you might like a copy after reading about all the problems you've had with your hair. Black people have a terrible preoccupation with hair because of our four hundred years without a comb," she explained.

"I'm not sure I understand."

"We didn't have a comb. We couldn't comb our hair with European combs so we were poorly groomed and self-conscious about our hair. That's why we resorted to all sorts of things to make us look better. Bacon fat to make it lie down—we didn't have anything else. Rags to cover it up. All because we didn't have a comb."

"You mean an Afro pick?"

"Yes," she said.

"Well, we've got the comb now."

"But we haven't changed our behavior. As a braider, I'm trying to get black women to give up these harsh chemicals and go back to natural hairstyles," she said.

I like braids, I told her. For the past thirteen years, when my hair wasn't in an Afro, it had been cornrowed. But I got tired of both styles. Besides, I told her, "the cornrows were tight. They either gave me a headache or made my head itch."

"Ohhhh," she cooed, "then you'd love the individual braids. No tension on the scalp. Great styling versatility."

"How much is it?" I asked.

"Four hundred dollars."

"What!"

"Oh, it takes a great deal of skill and time. It's an art. I take credit cards. And if you don't have cash, I'm not locked into this capitalist system. We can barter. Or, you can give me something as collateral. Do you have any jewelry or African art?"

"Well," I said, watching her braid as we talked—she did do beautiful work, "I have some Makonde statues I brought back from Tanzania."

"I'd love to see those," she said.

I noticed she had several pieces of beautiful African art in the shop already. I wondered if one ever got one's "collateral" back from her.

"No," I said, musing, "I wouldn't want to put up my African art as collateral."

"What else do you have?"

"I've got that famous photograph of Billie Holiday at her last recording session, shot by Milt Hinton."

"I'd love to see that," she said eagerly.

I gave in eventually, but I never put up any of my art as collateral.

The price of a good braider has dropped since then. The one I have in Los Angeles now is reliable and reasonably priced. She works out of her home—I like that. And when we take breaks—braiding is an all-day affair—we make an indoor picnic out of it. It reminds me a little of the old days and Mrs. Lane.

You can't get hot goods at my braider's house, but she makes up for it with great stories. Like the one about her friend who checks insurance claims. One claim was for a lady who'd been rushed to the emergency room to have a potato removed. The woman told the doctor she'd been in her garden that night digging up potatoes and fell on one. The potatoectomy—from the woman's most intimate bodily orifice—went unchallenged by the insurance company. Even though the raw tuber was completely peeled when retrieved.

I never heard anything that good in Mrs. Lane's shop.

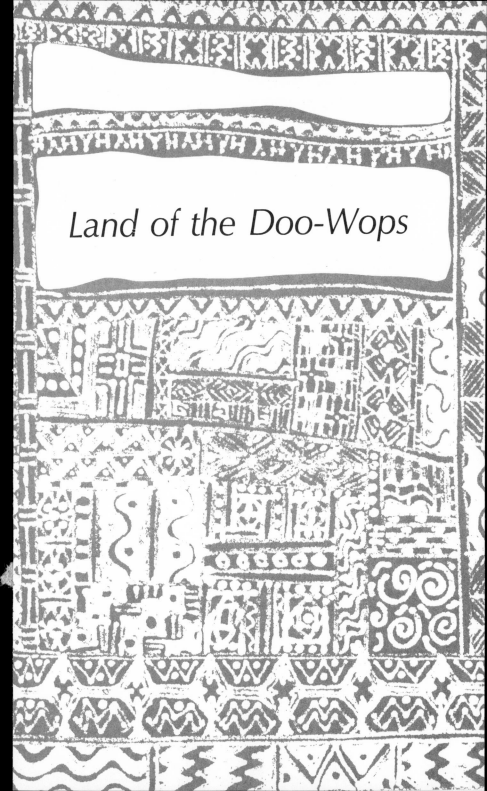

# Land of the Doo-Wops

etween lunch, dinner and a high-speed motorbike ride through the hills of Hamilton, Bermuda, I'd had sixteen screwdrivers. It wasn't my intention to have sixteen screwdrivers, get onstage and fall off the stage into Rosie Grier's lap. But by the time I reached Bermuda, the act I was in had hit every region of the United States in a series of mostly one-night stands with a minor talent named Major Harris.

You remember Major, once a member of the Delfonics, once high on the record charts as a soloist with the 1975 hit "Love Won't Let Me Wait." You can still get it in record stores or in a collection of Top 40 pop for lovers advertised on late-night TV and available through the mail with your VISA or MasterCard. The record was most notable for the orgasmic moaning of an anonymous background singer. It wasn't me.

The background singers on the record were replaced with the three members of a hastily thrown together group called Brown Sugar. I was the crystal on the left.

Brown Sugar had problems. Angela, a childhood friend, did too many drugs and was always hoarse. Candi, who was beautiful, had a tiny voice and hated singing heavy rhythm and blues—which really wasn't what we were doing, but what we did was still too gutbucket for her. And I hadn't been back in the real world long.

I had gone from opera to jazz to political theater with the Spirit House Movers, playwright Amiri Baraka's theater company, and Blakluv, a theater group I co-founded in Boston. I was unaccustomed to the world of commercial entertainment. And I definitely was not used to singing anything but lead.

"You take the next solo," Barry Manilow said. I launched into "Heat Wave" and blew away the competition at the audition—I thought. Manilow called me at home and gave me the nicest rejection I ever received as a performer. But I knew what the problem was before he opened his mouth. I was fine as a soloist. But background singing is an ensemble art, and one has to blend, not stand out. When he listened to me with the other two singers, my vibrato could be heard above everyone else, he said.

But I was willing to bottle my voice and my ego as part of Brown Sugar. I may have had the best pipes in the group, but doo-wop artistry was new to me, as well as the life-style that accompanied it. I was willing to look, listen and learn. I was also content to let Angela assume control of the group. She had been a touring backup singer for years, as she constantly reminded me. And her ears were better attuned to the collective art we were practicing. She could "help me" spot and squelch my occasional lapses into operatic style. She took delight in telling me this, now that I was performing on her turf. Angela had felt the need to compete with me since the day we met in high school.

We both attended Music and Art. I won the school's top vocal music award the year I graduated. Angela flunked out and had to go to another high school. I made my debut at Carnegie recital hall when I was sixteen. I'd been named best new pop vocalist in the 1969 equivalent of *Star Search*, a talent show at the Brooklyn Academy of Music sponsored by M-G-M Records and Metromedia Television in New York.

A talent scout claiming to represent Motown came backstage after the show and said he wanted me to cut a demo. Whether he was for real or not, I don't know, but in my youthful wisdom, I primly said: "No thank you. I intend to be an opera singer."

"Is Leontyne Price ready?" I heard Angela ask, as we prepared to open for the Ohio Players and the Spinners. I was twenty-three and the one-night stands were killing my voice.

I could move well onstage, but had great difficulty following a set pattern of steps. ("They're not going to ask you to dance, are they?" my own mother wanted to know when I got the job.) When Angela and Candi turned left, I swung to the right. When they were facing front, I was facing back.

One night, on the stage of a packed Shreveport, Louisiana, arena, we stepped up to our microphones dressed in royal blue satin gowns, the backs cut to just above the derriere, a touch of pale blue ostrich feathers clinging to the plunging halter necklines. With our pelvises swirling and some fancy variations on the cha-cha, we finished the last "*Ooh ooh, loving you is mellow*" riff, a line from a nonhit Major Harris tune of the same name. Then came the opening strains of the song for which the audience had been clamoring, "Love Won't Let Me Wait."

"*The time is right, you hold me tight, and love's got me high,*" Major sang. The young girls in the audience, barely past puberty, shrieked in ecstasy. "*Please tell me yes.*"

"*Yes,*" Brown Sugar whispered in response, after navigating a choreographed turn that placed us in front of the microphone at the appropriate moment. I got there first. But I was in step that time; Angela and Candi were behind the beat. The three of us eyed each other evilly in an attempt to escape blame.

As the tune arched toward a climax, Major sang, "*Now move*

*a little close to me. You owe it to yourself. And I will selfishly take a little for myself. . . ."* Then Angela moaned in mock ecstasy while we vamped, *"Love won't let me wait,"* and Major crooned, *"Temperature's rising, 'cause you're so tantalizing. . . . Love won't let me way-ay-ait. . . ."*

Angela dropped her head slightly as she groaned and looked at me sideways for approval. I wouldn't moan onstage, but I'd been coaching her to take the girlish grin off her face, the whine out of her voice, and moan like a woman. I half rolled my eyes at her; she still didn't have it down.

In the middle of the next song, I heard a "pssst, pssst, pssst" from the wings. I couldn't figure out what the road manager was trying to say, but I could tell he was trying to say it to me. We did a quick turn and a chorus of deep-voiced "Yeahs" rose from the audience. The hook on the low back of my royal blue gown had come undone, exposing the major portion of my derriere. One of the Spinners came onstage and hooked me up while I smiled wide to the applause and kept misstepping.

Major's record producers checked out the show in Miami. They were not crazy about Brown Sugar's sound. We didn't do Major's big L.A. concert. But we joined him in Bermuda. He stayed in a big, fancy hotel. We stayed two steps up from a dump.

I was depressed. I went bike riding with the concert promoter. At every stop, he told the bartender I was one of the "girls" in the show. We were always called girls. Background singers who are fifty are called girls. I considered it sexist and demeaning and asked the men on the tour not to call me that, much to Angela's annoyance. "This is show business," she said. But "girls" and "show" were all the island bartenders had to hear to fill for free my half-empty glass before I knew it.

By the time I went on the stage of the Zodiac Club, I was

seriously wopped. And when I sang my third or fourth doo and misstepped that night, I fell into football giant Roosevelt Grier's lap. He picked me up, put me back onstage and I kept going.

But it wasn't Brown Sugar's mismatched voices or my failure to master the simplest dance steps that did us in.

One of Major's producers had come with the show to Bermuda. He had the hots for Candi. She wasn't called Candi for nothing. He drove her to an isolated beach. He told his chauffeur to come back in the morning. They struggled on the beach. She kicked him in the groin. They had to walk back to Hamilton. It took all night, though I don't recall the beach being that far from town. I guess he limped most of the way.

We got canned the next day. We had plane tickets back to the States but no money. We hadn't been paid for several weeks.

I told Major I was broke. He gave me two hundred dollars cash and said he liked me, liked my voice, liked the way I carried myself. Look him up when I get back home.

I looked him up for the rest of my money. I went to the record company in Philadelphia with the rest of Brown Sugar. I told Angela, our designated manager, to get out of my face when she failed to get our funds in Philly, then I took over.

Major was in Cherry Hill, New Jersey, we were told. We got a lift with the band and Major's sleazy brother-in-law roadie.

In New Jersey, the sleaze tried to keep me from seeing Major and started wagging his finger in my face. I jumped at him, pushed him aside and dared him to lay a hand on me.

The guys in the band, their noses pressed against their car windows, watched me with shocked expressions. I'd been the least assertive member of Brown Sugar, but only because the road experience was new to me. The sleaze said he was going to talk to Major. He came back a few minutes later and said the star would see me. One of the band members rolled down the car window. "You can represent me anytime," he said.

I saw Major and got our money.

At the end of the "Love Won't Let Me Wait" tour, I decided I hadn't spent my life studying music to put up with the crap I'd experienced *and* sing music I didn't like. I wanted to sing jazz—that's what I'd been doing in Boston during college—and I decided to return to it. I put together material for an act and started perfecting it in showcase performances at New York clubs.

At the same time, Angela—we were still talking—had arranged to get studio work for us as background singers. Neither of us was making enough money, though. She suggested we tour again. Out of financial desperation, I told her I'd think about it.

I didn't have to sing for a living if I didn't want to, however. I'd decided my second year in college to drop music as my major and get my degree in communications—always have something to fall back on, my mother told me. I had worked as a broadcast journalist right after college. But I missed singing; it is the most immediate kind of creative expression. I sang first and foremost just for the joy of it. When all else seemed to fail me during a very troubled adolescence, there was always music. It was my religion—an unrealistic perspective for an entertainer. In this country music is, above all else, a business. And until one attains clout in that business, other people dictate what one sings and how one sings it. I considered that messing with my religion. But this was the reality I had to confront whether I was singing Top 40 or jazz.

I still hadn't decided what I was going to do professionally when my agent called. I had an audition to join the road company of *Bubblin' Brown Sugar*, she said—oh no, I was wary of anything with Brown Sugar in the name. I told her I'd think about it.

In the meantime, I had two other auditions set up, one with the manager of an act I had met while touring with Major Harris, the other with Luther Vandross.

The Vandross audition took place in his New York apartment a few years before he became a stellar soul balladeer. He was very friendly and down-to-earth. I'd brought my own accompanist, Richard Cummings, a childhood friend who has been Harry Belafonte's musical director for years. He is a sensitive pianist and arranger, and I'd asked him to write a soulful, torchy arrangement of "You and Me Against the World." Vandross loved it. But he wanted me to come back for a final audition with the other singers. "I want to hear how you blend," he said.

The next day I went to the manager of the group I'd met while touring with Major. We talked for a few minutes in a large, empty office in a midtown Manhattan skyscraper. I thought it a strange place for an audition. "I've heard you, I know you can sing," he said. "But we need more than a singer." He abruptly excused himself, said he'd be back in a moment and went into an adjoining room. Well, if he wants a singer who can dance, it's all over, I thought.

He called me from the other room. When I walked in, he was sitting naked on the desk. "I'd like to make a film with you," he said, standing now, smiling.

I really didn't think stuff this gross happened outside the movies. He was a very short man.

I smiled back, moved toward him slowly, put my arms around his neck and kneed him in the groin.

When Vandross called me for the second audition, I told him I wasn't interested. When I called my agent, I told her to forget about *Bubblin' Brown Sugar*. Then I put my application to Columbia University's School of Journalism in the mail.

I don't think I would have had much of a future as a background singer in any case. I kept hearing rumors about me from people still in the business: "That girl, she's got a real attitude problem."

# What's Love Got to Do with It?

*T*he beautiful woman was half naked and running. She sped down Convent Avenue past a row of tenements on one side, City College on the other, her ponytail flying behind her, her spotless white panties and white bra hugging the most private parts of her cinnamon-colored body. Her feet were bare, her thighs were powerful, her legs were long, her knees came near the tips of her rocket breasts as she propelled herself over curbs, ignoring DON'T WALK signs, escaping sure, but to me unseen, danger.

She disregarded Satchel Paige's timeless warning and looked over her shoulder in the next block, losing momentum. If someone was gaining on her, I couldn't make it out. She picked up speed and disappeared down the avenue while I stood on the corner biting a dill pickle, eating from a bag of barbecue potato chips, stupidly staring at her vanishing cloud of cinnamon dust. Why, I wondered, did the beautiful lady have no clothes on? Why was she running? Who could she be running from? It was summer. I was ten. It was all a mystery to me.

It is spring. I am twenty-eight. I have met Nick. Why the cinnamon lady vanished is less a mystery to me now.

• • •

I got a present for my birthday. "You're pregnant," the doctor said. My face froze and then I laughed soundlessly. The doctor smiled.

"What about my blocked tubes?" I asked, knowing it was a stupid question now.

"Well, at least one of them is unblocked now," she told me, and said wasn't it "wonderful" to know I could get pregnant after all.

I was silent.

"You and the father should talk this over and make plans for the baby," she futilely encouraged. My face told her what my plans were.

Years before, I'd had a misdiagnosed case of pelvic inflammatory disease. By the time the doctors realized what it was, the infection had left masses of scar tissue in and around my fallopian tubes. The surgeon who operated on me thought it improbable that I'd ever have children. I stopped taking the pill and for years had relied on other forms of birth control successfully—the diaphragm, foams, jellies, and those few "safe" days each month. It was on a safe night, when the moon was full over Miami, that I got pregnant. Dumb.

But I wasn't about to compound my error. I wanted a child one day, but I didn't want one then and I didn't want one by Nicholas Wright. It was a full moon that made me do it and I was infatuated with another man, a thousand miles away.

"I am quite sure that I want an abortion," I told the doctor.

She stiffened. "If you decide to do that, I'll have to refer you to another physician. I don't do abortions," she said, "and I don't think you should have one."

I rolled my tongue around the front of my teeth and said, "Ah-huh." My paper gown crinkled as she put her arm across my shoulders.

# What's Love Got to Do With It?

"Talk it over with the baby's father," she said softly.

As I got dressed, I chose to focus all my rage on her. How dare she tell me not to have an abortion. But I'd seen all those bad movies about this situation and knew I should at least discuss my plans with Nicholas.

I went back to work. I felt sleepy. Everything nauseated me. I got up from my computer terminal in the newsroom and headed for the bathroom. I walked differently. My pelvis seemed to jut forward more, my thin hips felt loaded with sacks and swayed with the momentum of women I'd seen twice my size. I was almost twelve weeks pregnant and, despite the nausea, liked the feeling. I sat in the bathroom stall considering how great it was to carry the future within you. That I could have a baby after all did thrill me, and I worried if aborting this child would endanger my chances of having another.

I don't remember how many days passed before I told Nick. But when I called him, he was at work, at one of the paper's satellite offices near my apartment.

"I need to talk to you."

"What's the matter?" he said.

"I just need to talk to you."

"Can't you tell me on the phone what's the matter? I'm real busy."

I held the phone from my ear and looked at the kitchen ceiling. Is this man going to be a total jerk? "I need to talk to you about this in person," I went on. Hadn't he seen the movies? Did I have to spell it out? See, he was going to be just the ass I expected. Why bother telling him? My better judgment had kept him at bay for over a year. I only succumbed under the power of a full moon, and when it's full, it's even fuller in Miami, often looking like a harvest moon, poised low on the horizon, skimming the surface of the Atlantic.

"Can you at least give me an indication of what this is about?"

he asked, like a man who knows exactly what this is about.

"All right, Nicholas, whenever."

"Okay, okay, I'll be over as soon as I can."

I was sleepy; I was depressed. I was throwing up. I went back to bed and left the apartment door open. He walked through it less than half an hour after I'd hung up the phone.

I said something about the swiftness of his arrival while he looked at me warily. "Why is the door open?"

"So I wouldn't have to get up to let you in," I said sullenly. I was sitting up in the bed, my arms wrapped around my stomach. He walked around the bed and sat in a chair beside me.

I looked straight ahead instead of at him. "I am pregnant. You are the father." I waited half a beat for him to say something louselike here. He didn't. "I thought it only right to discuss with you what I'm going to do." I addressed him with the impersonal hostility of a prosecutor offering a plea bargain to a known crook. "Next Saturday, I am going to have an abortion. I would like you to pick me up that morning, take me to the hospital, wait for me then bring me home. Since I make more money than you, I will pay for any costs not covered by my insurance." I breathed in deeply then let it out with a shudder more internal than apparent.

I half turned to look at him. His hands were clasped and he nodded slightly. "You wanted to discuss this with me or just wanted to give me instructions?"

I tried a chuckle but it came out a faint snort. "Yeah, well, that's what I want you to do. Do you have any objections?" He shook his head. I got under the bed covers. "You reacted better than I thought," I mumbled, pressing the back of my head into the pillow and my backside into the mattress.

"You expected me to act like a jerk and just walk away?"

Why should he walk away? I had the no-fault plan all laid out. I was going to pay for it, too. All he had to do was drive the getaway car. If Nicholas knew someone else could and would take responsibility for everything, why should he make the effort to change anything? And I had made it easy.

Always Sir Charm, he became Prince Magnanimous now, too. "I wouldn't let you go through this alone."

He made me get up when he left. "Don't leave that door open again," he said.

"My husband doesn't know I'm here," a woman seated next to me said to another. She spoke with a Spanish accent and told the woman she had four children already. About a dozen of us sat in the hospital's abortion clinic anteroom. A slim redhead in her early twenties reassured an even younger-looking woman. "This is my third," she said. "It's nothing."

I got up and walked around the perimeter of the room. A door with a glass window separated us from waiting mothers, sisters, and various male liaisons. Nicholas sat with his head bent toward spread, bouncing knees. His arms rested on his thighs and his clasped hands periodically beat his forehead. I was surprised. I smiled.

They kept me at the hospital longer than usual, the nurses consoling me, a doctor holding my hand and talking to me for a very long time. I could not stop crying. I can think of few circumstances that would compel me to have an abortion again.

When I was home and comfortably in bed, Nicholas asked if I had everything I needed. I lied and said yes. That I thought stoicism a virtue and was emotionally incapable of saying I needed anyone may have been obvious to some, but it was not yet apparent to me. He left quickly. My bitterness imploded. It was cemented when I later learned the reason for his hurried exit: a plane flight, with the woman he'd been seeing regularly in Miami on it. While she was out of town, she had phoned to tell him she was pregnant too.

When this woman instigated a friendship with me—I knew I was being used but it gave me access to information about Nicholas—I discovered hers had been a hysterical pregnancy. By now, months had passed and Nicholas and I had formed a curious platonic friendship. It became evident that the abortion had been emotionally traumatic for both of us, and while he would not talk about it, it tied us to each other. Janice knew little about the history of our relationship, just that Nicholas and I were close. She'd been tapping all his friends lately for sympathy and information about Nick.

She called me in tears one Saturday, regurgitating Nicholas's latest emotional abuse. His continued womanizing had become intolerable, she said. After all, she had left another man for him—broken her engagement—after cheating on her fiancé with Nicholas for months, apparently.

I made my house call and sat in her living room nodding sympathetically at her travails. "Yes," I concurred, if Nicholas cocked his leg at a fire hydrant, I wouldn't be surprised. "And a bourgeois, emotional hustler," I added. "So what more do you want me to say, Janice? I can't tell you what to do. I know all of Nicholas's faults. That he and I are friends at all"—I paused—"well, it's a strange set of circumstances." She sniffed into a tissue and looked at me with wide, green, whatever-do-you-mean? eyes. I feigned a verbal fumble with a dismissive shake of my head and said nothing.

Then she dropped some pillow talk. Nicholas had told her about our sexual relationship—"he liked the strawberries and whipped cream" but he could take or leave the rest, she intimated. Then, to cement our camaraderie, she threw in that she knew the lack of sexual interest was mutual.

I smiled indulgently. "Nicholas," I said, "suffers from classic Don Juanism."

"I know he's immature," she said, and blew her nose. We were both older than Nick and she had several years on me. "With Larry," her former fiancé—she blinked several times, then tried to smooth a bent, pale-blond eyelash with her finger— "we were always entertaining interesting people with intellectual and artistic interests."

She and I knew Nicholas was no intellectual. But he was bright and quick-witted, and you don't need much more than that to be a competent journalist. Nicholas, however, had something extra—charisma. Lots of men liked him, too. He burst through the newsroom doors each day like a satisfied gunslinger—his sexual conquests notched on the handle of his six-shooter and one hand swinging a lariat of well-hung flesh instead of rope. At the time, I was glad few knew I'd been lassoed. But this Janice was dying to dig out the poop and I was glad for the opportunity to reciprocate her bitchiness. It would reveal my ties with Nick went beyond casual sex. I didn't count on it being replayed for a larger audience.

Nicholas came looking for me. "Where's little bigmouth?" he demanded, storming into my section of the newsroom. "She's not here," he claimed half a dozen people replied in unison.

He was seething when he found me. I think I was in the cafeteria. He whispered, "You said something to somebody that I don't think you should have said." Mr. No Sweat had a mad-on. I looked at him benignly.

"Janice confided her concerns to me and one thing led to another. It was my story to tell, too, if I chose. And I did."

"Did you choose to have her get drunk, stand outside my house at two A.M. and broadcast to the whole neighborhood: 'You got Itabari pregnant when I told you I was pregnant, too'?"

• • •

I don't remember how long Nicholas and I didn't speak to each other after that one. But within months, given the incestuous nature of journalism, I got involved with Janice's best friend, a television reporter with whom she worked. It soon became obvious that this was not going to work out and I suggested we end it. The man insisted he was willing to try anything to make it work. I went out of town on a story for several weeks and when I returned he was in a new relationship without having said a word. I was insulted but not particularly upset. Nicholas, of all people, was fuming. "I'm really pissed at the way this guy is treating Itabari," he admitted telling a mutual friend.

Then I started a wild affair with a man Nick thought dangerous. He warned me to be careful. I told him I would.

Nicholas had become the one to whom I told my secrets. And we laughed at each other's perversities.

He was seeing Debbie now, again, on and off. She was the one woman I believed he loved. I always thought they'd get married—when he was ready to get married, which I knew was a long way off. She was brainy, sensuous and, at that time, had a level of self-esteem several leagues beneath the sea. She worshiped Nick and seemed willing to endure whatever he did, albeit with the forlorn countenance of a wife shunned by her husband at every social event they attended. She was content to be the one he took home—most often.

Nicholas needed one woman on whom he could depend, someone who—after he'd outraged all the others—would give him unconditional love. And since we have social taboos regarding incest, he picked Debbie.

One night a group of us gave a good-bye party for a fellow journalist at a restaurant. The day before, it had been announced that I was leaving the paper for a year to accept a fellowship.

# What's Love Got to Do With It?

After dinner, Nicholas got up from the opposite end of the table where he'd been sitting with Debbie and put a chair next to me. He sat. "So you're actually leaving," he said incredulously, and shook his head. I nodded, then turned to talk to the person beside me. "So," he repeated, sounding marginally intelligent, "Itabari's really leaving."

"Yes, but I'll be back."

"You know, I'm . . . I'm going to miss you . . . really."

I gave him an aw-shucks smile, then turned away. Debbie had ground down an eighth of an inch of teeth trying to ignore us. I did not want her to think I was one of Nicholas's current side events. Our party was milling around the table. As soon as I got the opportunity I said to her, "Why don't you take my seat and let me work your end of the table? You belong in this spot anyway."

My impending departure emotionally panicked Nicholas. He wanted to spend time with me. He wanted to come visit me while I was on my fellowship.

I had to talk this through with Dr. J., my shrink. It took several weeks of emergency sessions.

One night in a bar I looked at Nick and spoke very carefully. "I can only speak for myself. I don't want to suggest that you . . . Let me begin again. I don't know about you, but I'm afraid of getting involved with you. It's not like before and I'm afraid of what I feel."

"I am too," he said, and reached across the table for my hand.

We had known each other for three years.

Not long after that night in the bar he wanted to go for a drink after work. We were both going to be at the paper late so I said I would.

Debbie walked in, planted herself at his desk and decided to wait for him. He came up behind me while I was reading a memo on the newsroom bulletin board. "I see your wife is here," I said without looking at him, "so forget it." I went straight home.

My phone rang after midnight. He was calling from a phone booth. Could he come over? Could he spend the night? He needed to be with me.

I told him no. He knew my position on being a side event. I minimally required equal billing if not star status. "Please . . ." he began to beg. This was getting difficult; Nick was not a pleader. I felt my legs. I hadn't shaved them. "No," I said firmly, running my hand across the stubble. Besides, I have an early day tomorrow, I told myself. And it's far too late to get up and shave, I told myself. And the house was a mess. . . . How frightened was I of this man?

At my healthiest, I sought men as friends and emotional partners. At my most neurotic, I had no use for them outside of sex. The disastrous model of my parents' marriage had taught me the erroneous lesson that men were obstacles; they just got in the way of everything a woman wanted and needed to do for herself. On the health-neurosis scale, I'd not yet found my equilibrium when I knew Nick.

I'd been a musician more of my professional life than a journalist, and it's easy to avoid commitments when you're on the road or the person you're seeing is in town for one week and won't be back for another six. (Actually, I've had similar relationships with lots of journalists, so having and being a vagabond lover was habitual.) In short, my career choices bolstered the myriad defenses I had erected to protect myself from rejection.

I was groaning the pronoun "I . . . I . . . I . . ." as Dr. J. watched. "I . . . guess . . . maybe, I might . . . love him." By the time the session was over I stumbled out deciding I did.

Since I believed in confronting one's demons—an appropriate term, I thought, for Nick—I had to act on this revelation. I sent him a bunch of balloons with a note stating: ". . . and by the way . . . I love you." Then I hid.

The spheres of hot air were flying high over his desk in the newsroom when I walked in. A walled corridor kept me out of sight for several feet until it became a half-walled partition on the left. He was on the phone and didn't notice me when I passed. My department was a good distance from his desk. I sat down at a computer terminal—not mine. I picked one farther out of sight, became a hunchback and started typing.

"What's the matter with you?" my friend Teresa, another reporter, asked. She eyed my lowered profile quizzically.

"I'm kind of hiding."

"I see." She sucked in her cheeks. "From anyone I know? I'm just inquiring so I can protect you from whomever it is."

"I'll tell you later."

"Nicholas was looking for you," she reported dryly. She didn't care for Nick. None of the sensible women I knew did. I looked around her to see the other side of the newsroom. Nicholas was off the phone. He got up. He got waylaid by an editor. I skulked off to the bathroom.

I tried to convince myself that I hadn't done anything so terrible—except to tell the cad of the decade what I really felt, just like all those other bimbettes. But it was done. I strode confidently out of the bathroom stall. I sat at my own desk. The phone rang.

"I got your balloons." He said nothing about the note.

"Ah-huh," I said. He invited me to dinner after work. I said, "Ah-huh." When he picked me up at my apartment, I let him in the door and said, "Hi, have a seat; I'll be right back," then rushed into the bedroom. When I came out, we rode down the elevator in silence. The doorman went to get Nick's car. Resembling a sad sack of potatoes, I dangerously sat on the dolly used for tenants' groceries.

"You don't look like you feel too well," he said.

"Hmmmm," I responded.

In the car I said less. Over dinner, little. At his apartment, he made love to me without saying he loved me. It all felt wrong.

Within weeks I learned Nicholas had been cheating on Debbie not only with me but with her former roommate too—both when the woman was her roommate and after.

The phone rang at my office desk. The voice was a hoarse whisper: "Itabari." I could hardly hear the person and I was on deadline.

"Who is this?" I demanded, my fingers pounding the computer keyboard.

"Itabari?"

"Yes," I answered gruffly.

"This is Nicholas. How much money do you have on you?"

"What's the matter with you? Where are you?" I looked at the clock.

He stopped whispering but mumbled as if his mouth was pressed hard against the receiver. "I'm at the police station."

"What did you do?" I inquired unsympathetically.

He had gone to the police station to examine some records for a news story. When he gave the officer his driver's license as identification, his name jumped out of the computer. He had hundreds of dollars in outstanding traffic tickets. They weren't going to let him leave the station until he paid up.

"Do you have a couple of hundred dollars?" he asked me.

"I haven't cashed my paycheck, I don't know what my balance is, and I don't have time to look now. And why do I get the royal honor of bailing you out? You've got a whole stable to choose from." The indignity of the ever-elegant Nicholas Wright being detained by police while playing ace reporter and dressed for a *GQ* cover was an image that fueled my writing speed. I beat my deadline just so I could hurry up and savor his humiliation at my leisure.

No one in the stable's inner circle bailed him out. He had to go to its periphery, a secretary at the paper.

I picked a fight and we stopped talking.

A month or more later, we made up.

In my apartment, the wall of bedroom windows overlooked Biscayne Bay. The moon was whole and low over the pitch-dark water. He was already in bed, his naked back to me, as I entered the room. I stood at the door. Where the curve of his waist dipped in then rose toward his hip, the moonlight fell, illuminating a spot of deep brown perfection. He was tall and looked longer in repose. He was firm and seemed harder prone. I'd never witnessed him so still, so much a sculptor's dream, so completely present. I feared no one else could fill my bed again. In the morning, each curve of his found a resting place in mine. Slow and weak he said, "Lady . . . you . . . feel . . . good . . ."

Lady? Outraged, I told my shrink: "Is that his catchall name for everyone he beds?" Perhaps I was misinterpreting his sentiments, Dr. J. suggested.

It was hard for me to be rational. I was now beyond mere lunar influences with Nicholas. Whenever he approached me, he was surrounded by a blue haze. He stood over me one day while I sat at my desk and asked me something. But I couldn't hear him. The inside of my head felt stuffed with cotton batting as I tried to fathom the meaning of the blue aura. Interrupting him, I finally said, "I can't stand this."

"You can't stand what?"

"Every time I look at you now you've got this damn blue cloud of smoke around you."

"Don't worry about it." He smiled smugly. "It's good for you." He wanted to see me that night.

"No. I don't want to see you—ever."

His face dropped. "You don't mean that."

"That really kills me, you with a wounded look." A reporter passed us to get to his desk. "I'll talk to you later," I told him.

Later became a series of missives from me—he never wrote—and delayed, elliptical responses from him. "It takes me a while to answer you because you always . . . you dissect." He stopped. "Let's just say you're not shallow and I have to think it over before I can respond," he explained.

My letters advanced the virtues of the examined life. Nicholas conceded that he had thought about seeing a therapist. His compulsive womanizing had hurt a lot of people, and I wondered out loud to him if he really liked women at all. He never followed through on the therapy, to my knowledge, and always conveyed the attitude that the women caused all the problems by their excessive demands—fidelity the primary one, of course.

But Nicholas wasn't married, there was no reason why he shouldn't be with whomever he wanted, I told him. He just wanted to be with everyone and was cavalier about who got hurt in the end.

Yet for all his sexual bravado, there was something emotionally very feminine about Nick. I mean that there was—in that psychological balance of yin and yang—a "feminine" malleability of soul, a profound desire to yield that revealed itself when he submitted to his deeper nature. Maybe it was just the child in him, ever ready to love and be loved. He seemed to know intuitively, I think, what a woman desires and how she desires it. But it was an ability used mainly to manipulate them. I sensed he feared that emotional surrender to another meant a plummet without end, or a destined crash. All that anxiety may have compelled much of his macho posturing. When I looked into his eyes I saw the tiniest pair of sneakers, poised for the emotional getaway. And he confessed that I triggered, unlike anyone else, images of surrender at the rose-covered cottage. Personally, I wouldn't live in such a place. I told Nick all I wanted was consistency in our relationship. He thought that would inevitably lead to marriage. I thought it would give me the opportunity to see if he was marriageable.

He admitted my unpredictability unnerved him; his inability to control me made him want to "shake my brains loose," he said. "And I'm just not used to being with a woman who doesn't let me do what I want to do," he conceded. Then, with a shiver your grandma told you meant someone was walking on your grave, he told me, "I don't want to love anybody."

I, however, was into the sweetness of surrender now. And if Nicholas didn't want to take our relationship for an exclusive test run, I was ready to move on. I was leaving for the University of Michigan in a few weeks to start my fellowship. I had a whole year to explore new territory. But first, I made a side trip.

The National Association of Black Journalists was holding its annual convention in Atlanta that year. I drove there on my way to Michigan. I thought it best to avoid Nicholas. We'd parted on good terms in Miami and I was content to leave it that way.

"Where have you been?" he asked at a cocktail party a couple of days into the convention.

I shrugged. "Around."

That night more than a dozen of us went to a popular Atlanta restaurant for dinner. We lingered over drinks in the lounge for a long time waiting to be seated. I was talking to a young reporter from Miami named Alex. At the time, I thought he was far too young for me. "But I'll grow up," he told me one night at a similar gathering in Miami. Nicholas was there that night, too. Alex was charming, bright and sensitive. Nicholas could tell we liked each other and butted into our conversation.

"I know you," he whispered in my ear. "What do the two of you have planned tonight?" When he left the table, Alex looked at me incredulously. "You two really like each other. I don't get it. I don't see what women see in him."

Nick butted in again now at the Atlanta restaurant and deposited himself next to me. When our party was called for dinner he put himself at the head of the table with me beside him. I spent the whole evening trying to prevent him from pulling my underwear off from under the table.

When the bunch of us returned to the hotel, Nicholas got off the elevator when I did. "Where are you going?" I asked.

He mumbled like a little boy, "Wit-chu." What the hell, I was going away for a year.

I was in the bathroom, standing in front of the mirror, taking off my jewelry, when he came up behind me, his pants all undone. He pressed against me, his hands reaching and rubbing my thighs till the hem of my silk dress hung at my hips. His breath was in my ears and in my eyes when he whispered, "I love you, too." I looked at our reflection in the mirror. My mouth was open. "Say something," he pleaded.

I groaned a sound of pain, surprise and something like a baby dribbling. "I can't believe it," I mumbled.

"I've always loved you. I always thought you were the most wonderful, talented, exciting woman I ever met . . ."

In the night I said, "I need you."

In the dark he said, "You got me."

And then there was a long silence.

A month into the silence I called him. "You didn't mean it," I said.

"Don't tell me I didn't mean it. I meant it. I just have to think about what I'm going to do. I need a couple of weeks to think."

# What's Love Got to Do With It?

That was in September of one year. I didn't see him until October of the next. But I did see his parents.

I had met his father in Miami but never his mother. I had a standing invitation to visit them whenever I was in Chicago and did, for a long weekend. Nicholas was an only child and his bedroom had been turned into a shrine—elementary school, high school and college mementos everywhere. His father suggested the room be used as office space, but his mother kept it ready for Nick, just in case he wanted to move back home, she said.

Over breakfast, she told me, "Nicholas has been telling us about you for years. How wonderful you are. How . . ." In short, everything he had whispered to me that night in Atlanta.

And then I met a man he'd grown up with, went to college with, at a party while I was in Michigan. We'd been chatting for several minutes when he said, "Wait, you're here on a fellowship and you're from Miami? Is your name Itabari?" I told him it was and he proceeded to tell me my life history and everything about me but what size underwear I wore. But no word from Nick.

I had a great year and returned to Miami with two goals: finish a book and avoid Nicholas Wright.

It was useless to stay in a constant state of rage with Nick. I decided to be civil at all times but distant.

I'd been back a couple of months and the first complete sentence he spoke was "Could I borrow some money?" It was an insignificant amount and he said he'd give me a check and it would clear in a week and blah blah blah. I told him I was busy and to call me at home later. "What's your number?" he asked. I'd been back two months and he was asking me my number. That sealed it. I knew all this was a test to see if I was still on the emotional hook. I would have said no anyhow. But I did it with decorative venom when he called. "Go to a loan shark, motherfucker. With your repayment record, my prayers will be answered."

Every time I saw his head pop up in the newsroom, I felt my right eyelid twitch and my stomach knot. But I stored the venom. I couldn't let him distract me from my book.

He struck again about a month later. He wanted my opinion on a political matter and suggested a late lunch. It became an early dinner.

A master of the amnesiac's stare, he gazed at me from across the table, then gave me the *Gaslight* treatment. "What do you mean about the last time we were together? I thought the last time we were together everything was cool." I had dished up the past after he served the bullshit pretext for the dinner.

"You know, Nicholas," I began softly and with a smile, "nothing has changed. I still love you, unfortunately. I just don't respect you. I never did, really. You're a man for whom the past never happened, the present doesn't matter and the future never comes." And then I vowed to myself: I'm going to teach him the meaning of the Word. The pen is mightier than the penis. But before I would get to that, there were scenes to be played.

The bill came and, mealymouthed, he said something about just having enough to pay his half of the bill. "I'm glad you do," I said quietly, and watched him count out twenty-two pennies.

On the way back to the paper, we passed the company parking lot. I glanced across the hedges at my Mustang. In its trunk, wrapped in a finger towel, was a knife with a lovely black handle. It was not an uncommon knife; you could find it among the better cutlery at any K mart—in fact, I think that's where I bought mine. Meant simply for the mundane chores of paring, it was beautifully designed, sculpted to fit the pinky where the handle curved inward an inch from the end. From there it rose toward the center, where it arched to cushion the middle fingers, then dipped inward again to fit the index finger. It was perfect for skinning a peach, peeling a potato or a quick, low-hand thrust to the groin.

I had put the knife in the trunk after Nicholas requested money and then my phone number so he could delineate his plea.

As we rode up the escalator, my mood seemed mellow, my face serene. I asked Nicholas if he was still seeing Debbie. "Just as a friend," he said quietly. He looked at me with big, apologetic eyes, one of the more obvious ploys in his arsenal of body language designed to avoid the commitment of words. The amnesiac's stare was now replaced by a soulful, liquid gaze, from which I was to surmise his regret and continued affection. I said nothing either. And if my gestures spoke resignation and goodwill while my mind plotted dismemberment and disposal, what deception could he think possible? For rather than seethe and strike without warning, hadn't I always been the snake that rattled, the one who verbalized and dissected his feelings and mine, his motivations and mine, ad infinitum? As we walked through the corridor, he looked sad. My angelic countenance radiated both love and the realization that some lovers are forever estranged. There was no reason to distrust me. Toward him, my word and deed had been one. For me to behave otherwise would have been, to him, unthinkable. I was into my soap opera mode now.

I'd been back in Miami—the most socially desolate outpost in America for black people, but a great news town because so much bad happens there—for four months. Between work at the paper and my own writing, I hadn't had much time to socialize. But when I put my manuscript aside and looked around, I was bored. When I'm bored, I manufacture my own entertainment if there's none to be found. *You write the script, you direct the play and you star in the show*, Dr. J had cautioned. Nicholas was going to be my entertainment.

Weeks passed and he made friendly overtures. "I really like the way you come in to work, all business—your own business—" He added pointedly, "Then go home."

I looked up from my computer. "I'm so glad you approve of my behavior."

"You know," he began a few weeks later, "I don't think I like the way you just come in to work, have nothing to say, then leave." So we talked.

One afternoon he came by my apartment. I assumed the attitude of a *Dynasty* bitch looking over her lover's shoulder and smiling villainously, strains of "What's Love Got to Do with It" playing in her head. Nothing he did would hurt as much if I played this out as high-camp soap.

"You look really tired," he told me, observing me in profile. I was sorting through a stack of records and I *was* tired. It takes a lot of psychic energy to maintain a mad-on. He was sitting on the sofa and leaned toward me on the floor. "Whenever you wanted to reach out to me," he said quickly, "I . . . I acted like a bastard. Whenever I wanted to reach out to you, you acted like a bitch." Well, that was half the truth. He started to say more but I got up and left the room.

I talked to my reflection in the bathroom mirror. "Too late. I'm not going for it." My nose was red and my eyes were puffy. I threw cold water on my face, then went back to the living room.

"Nicholas, why are you here, why are you doing this?" I stood staring at him.

"I don't know," he mumbled, then pulled me toward him, then down on the sofa, and then he kissed my face and neck gently. I pulled away and eased myself to the floor. I looked at an album cover for a long time while we both said nothing. "Don't do that," he said, and pulled me back on the couch. He wiped the wetness from my cheek with his hand then held me. "I don't want to, but I have to go," he said after the stillness had settled us. "I'd rather be with you than . . . but I have to go. I'm in this situation . . . but it's not going to last much longer . . ."

Whoever it was, whatever it was, it was going to be a replay. No words passed my lips, no expression played across my face. He went to the bathroom. When he opened the door to leave it, I blocked his path. History had taught me he was most vulnerable in the can. I wrapped my arms around him and kissed him hard; he had trouble walking to the front door. "Women don't have this problem," he half groaned, half spoke. He stood there a few minutes trying to straighten up. I smiled, then kissed him hard again. I opened the door and he walked out stiffly. About a minute later, I looked through the peephole and saw him still standing there, shaking his head like he'd been smacked upside it and blessed quite suddenly with total recall. He was going to have a lot more to remember.

We both had to be in New York on business the following week and planned to meet for dinner and go to the theater. He left for New York before I did, but I didn't remember if he was leaving town on Thursday or Friday. We'd seen each other at work, but not after hours, since the afternoon in my apartment. I called him Thursday night to say how much I was looking forward to seeing him in New York Saturday. A woman answered the phone.

Nicholas had not delineated the "situation" he was in, but it must have been unique. Nick had stay-overs, but not live-ins. This had serious implications. I'd been waiting for him to do something that would push me over the edge, and she was it. I was feverish—emotionally and clinically hot. I had the flu. I hung up the phone, the woman's bovine voice still resonating moolike in my head. "Hel-lo," she'd answered lazily.

I got up from my bed and, through the window, saw the full, giant moon skimming the Atlantic. I went to the kitchen, where I'd stored an empty champagne bottle, its neck perfectly suited to slip into the gas tank of a little red Alfa Romeo. I went down to my garage to get the beautiful black-handled knife from my trunk—a perfect implement for ripping the cloth top of a convertible.

In the kitchen, I filled the champagne bottle with sugar. The inside of the bottle was wet. I'd washed it out. The sugar stuck. I threw the bottle away. I took the whole canister of sugar and a plastic measuring cup and put them in a small peach-colored shopping bag with the name of one of Miami's better department stores, Jordan Marsh, printed on it. I wrapped the black-handled knife in a paper towel and placed it in the bag, too.

Then I got my clothes for the evening. It was winter in Miami—that meant 70 degrees at night. I pulled out a black ski mask, a black long-sleeved turtleneck, baggy black cotton slacks, black high-top sneakers and short black wool gloves. It was nearly 11:00 P.M. I went to case his house.

I parked around the corner from his low-rise apartment building. His car was parked in a space directly in front of his living room window. Another car was parked behind it. I peeped in the window. She was full-bodied if not actually bovine and seated on the sofa watching the late news. I marched into the apartment lobby and stood outside his door, sans ski mask. I huffed up and I puffed up and then I thought it wise not to pound the door down. I listened a few seconds to the TV. Yeah, she was in there all right. I'd be back.

I drove home, took a few shots of Vicks Formula 44 for my cough, then set the alarm for 3:00 A.M. It would take twenty minutes to get to his apartment. I decided that the cow and the rest of the neighborhood would be in a deep REM phase of sleep between 3:30 and 4:00 in the morning on a weeknight.

At 3:35 A.M. I parked my car under a tree in an open, unpaved lot directly across from his building. As I opened my 1978 Mustang's door, the hinges *squeeeeeeeeaked* and the interior light illuminated my black-clad figure. Grimacing, I flicked off the light. I grabbed my chic peach satchel and eased the door open again. It squeaked even louder and I closed it as quickly as I could without slamming it. I rushed on sneakered feet to his car. His lot was illuminated by bright spotlights, one of them aimed directly at his car. I went to open the gas tank. It was locked. I'd forgotten. I pulled out the knife. The left side of his car faced the street but was hidden by another parked car. I went for the front left tire first. I stopped. I heard a car. But there was no car. I had never done anything like this before. I'd dismissed as childish and irrational all those women I'd ever heard of, seen or read about who busted up the "other woman" in some smoky nightclub, pulverized her on her own living room floor à la Mrs. Lionel Ritchie, or done what that really bad sister had: turned Al Green to grits and made him get religion all over again. Unlike those women, I couldn't admit that I cared enough to enter the emotional fray. But here I was about to stab this man's car, which I actually imagined to be a red Alfa Romeo given to him by one of the older, generous women he once told me about. That it was actually a Honda Civic hatchback made no difference. With his wrecked finances the damage would be just as painful. I raised the knife and plunged it in. *Poowwwwwwwwww!* I ran with my mouth open and eyes bulging back to my car. I'd never heard a stabbed tire explode. Sounded like a Beirut car bomb on the late news. "Whewwww," I whispered to myself.

*You write the script, you direct the play, you star in the show.*

"Hmmmmmmm." I envisioned a Miami cop catching me in

the act and arresting me. The *Herald* would send its ace cop reporter, the famous Edna Buchanan, to write a story about one of their own getting busted for a romantically motivated deed of banal vengeance. Edna would get that it was a reciprocal act of trust betrayed. Maybe. I decided the script called for me to go now.

I was ten minutes from the crime scene when I stopped my car on a side street. I was coughing so hard I thought I'd choke. When I finally stopped, I leaned on the steering wheel trying to catch my breath. "You got up out of bed to put a hole in one tire?" My ten-year-old self was sitting beside me in the front seat. She looked at me as dumbly as she had at the vanishing dust of the half-naked cinnamon lady, then bit off a piece of pickle. Her toe kicked a clump of knitted black wool on the car floor. I had thrown the ski mask there. Cellophane crackled as she dug into a bag of barbecue potato chips. She crunched one. "How come you had this hot thing on your head?" she asked, toeing the ski mask. I started coughing again and could not stop for half a minute or more. My eyes were watery, my face was red and a veil of perspiration hung around my forehead and temples. "You look bad," she said as she chewed a chip.

I sucked my teeth. "Girl, shut up. You ain't never loved a man." Then I drove back and stabbed all the other tires.

To this day, Nicholas doesn't know for certain that I was the tire slasher in the night, so along with this book, I'm sending him four Goodyear radials.

As for all those women who have been his, read this, suck their teeth, then say: "Shhh, he didn't tell her anything he didn't tell me," all I have to say is: *MAY*-be, but *my* version gets immortalized 'cause I can write it so good.

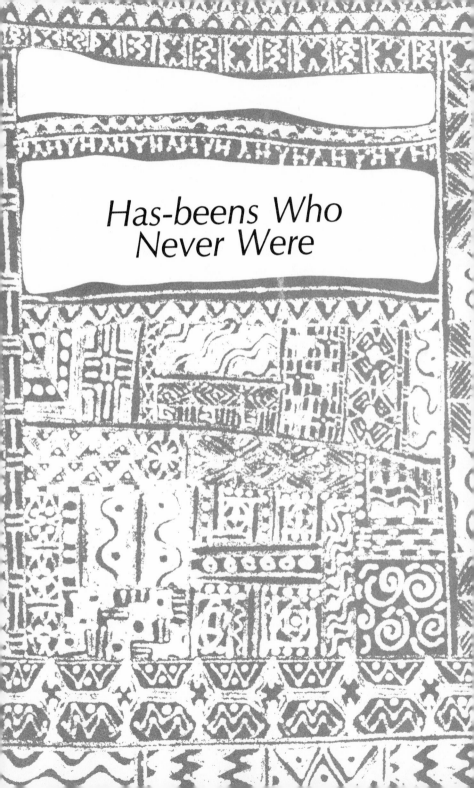

# Has-beens Who
# Never Were

A man I have not seen for fifteen years is telling a room full of strangers about my past.

I suppose many among the crowd already know me in an impersonal way. They have seen my byline in the *Miami Herald* and paused out of curiosity at the double consonants—even if they did not go on to read what was under it: offbeat feature stories, unusual first-person tales of my dysfunctional family, and reviews and essays about the arts. I have never, except to my employers, made known my credentials for assuming the role of critic. But this man, whom I've not seen since my adolescence, is, unexpectedly, about to expose bits of my curriculum vitae. And I don't like it.

"You shouldn't fear," he tells them, "that your children's future will be limited if they go to a school for the arts." This man, with the *Fame* logo pinned to his lapel, possesses the same gentle, soft-spoken manner I remember as a teenager; though my classmates and I at the High School of Music and Art gave Richard Klein lots of cause to lose his cool. The painter and administrator began his tenure as principal of the school that inspired the movie *Fame* as a man under siege.

Virtually every college campus in America in the late sixties and early seventies was lit by the fire of revolutionary rhetoric and defiant, nonconformist behavior. I was only in high school, but it was a school full of congenital nonconformists. Janice Ian ("Society's Child" and "At Seventeen") epitomized it. The image of her haunting the corridors between the school's Gothic walls has never left me: silent, her eyes cast down, her body bending in on itself, the retracting form intent on reclaiming its fetal posture.

But as soon as one passed that portrait of near catatonia, Liz Abzug (Bella-the-hat's daughter) would appear, lecture me in animated tones on leftist politics, then pronounce me a "Negro" because of my button-down-collar blouses, straightened hair, disdain for pot and support for liberal Republican John Lindsay in the upcoming mayoral election.

Across the street from our high school campus, Black Panthers at City College were protesting, with others, U.S. racism at home and imperialism abroad: Get out of Vietnam. End U.S. support for South Africa. And a few blocks farther away, more of the same was going on at Columbia University.

It did not take me long to get caught up in the political fervor. I was sixteen. I wanted the approval of my peers and, appropriate to the age, was breaking out of the world defined for me by my parents, both of whom were essentially Victorian. No matter that my father was a proclaimed Marxist whose library helped to fuel my natural intellectual curiosity and filled me, early in life, with ideas that challenged the political status quo. Or that my mother was fundamentally liberal in her style of parenting.

My father, after all, was born at the beginning of the twentieth century, went to the "Oxford" of Canada, the University of Toronto, and before that the bastion of Negro middle-class elitism, Morehouse. Further, true to the Victorian tradition, he believed that a patriarch was to be respected and served without challenge by the women and children in his household.

# Has-beens Who Never Were

My mother's sensibilities were shaped by parents born in the British colonial empire *during* Victoria's reign. She's a product of Catholic schools, as well. While she received a fine education in these schools, she also learned from the nuns the dreaded Mother Superior pose, which she still assumes—lips pursed, shoulders back, spine stiff, crossed hands on her abdomen—when confronted with anything she finds distasteful. Bessie Smith, for instance. Having discovered her at sixteen, I dragged my mother into the living room to hear one of Bessie's blues and was frozen by my mother's contempt: "Why would you bring me in here to listen to anything as vulgar as a woman singing about her jelly roll?"

I watched my mother press her lips into oblivion, then walk away with a stiff back. I didn't get it. I just loved Bessie's voice. I didn't know there was anything bad about jelly or a roll.

Culturally—like most middle-class non-WASPs of their generation who sought any degree of mainstream acceptance—one assimilated the cultural assumptions of Euro-America no matter how destructive to colored people's psyche. And the image of mainstream society most assimilationist blacks held was usually the most conservative—the safest, most proper conduct. After all, you're black, don't do anything else to stand out.

I was getting ready to stand out.

Richard Klein was present at the metamorphosis, mine and thousands of others'. That he didn't confuse me with all the rest, fifteen years later, is partly happenstance. He has come to Miami to tout the New World School of the Arts to parents and community leaders several months before he assumes the job of provost of the new school. I am covering the story for the paper. Interviewing this figure from my past turns out to be my last assignment for the *Herald*. In a few weeks, I will join the staff of the *Los Angeles Times* and begin a new phase in my career as a writer.

That I am now Itabari and not Jill should add all the more to his confusion about who I am, out of the thousands who swarmed through the six-story school that housed so much teenage energy, creativity and despair.

But he claims particular recall where I am concerned.

"An arts education," Klein tells the crowd, "increases your child's options in the world. It doesn't narrow them." Most of the students from Music and Art and Performing Arts (two different divisions of the same school, now called the LaGuardia School of the Arts) "do not become performers. They are doctors, teachers, lawyers, architects, writers. They receive both an arts education and a rigorous college preparatory education," he assures them.

"Right here, you have an outstanding journalist who could have had a great career in opera if she chose. She had one of the most beautiful voices of any student who ever came to the school. . . ."

I am an obvious blusher. Usually it's just my cheeks. But now I feel my earlobes turn hot. All who know me understand that I've never suffered from false modesty. But what sense is there in talking about a gift one failed to use as one might have, could have, should have? What is there to say about a "great" voice heard only by a limited public audience and a small circle of academics and professional musicians? The biggest crowds that heard me sing really came to hear the Ohio Players or the Spinners, for whom Major Harris was the opening act and I one of his mediocre background singers.

I stare at my reporter's pad as Klein speaks and gestures toward me. I hear the murmurs of surprise and know what will come.

"With a voice like that why didn't you do something with it?" one woman asks after Klein's speech.

I'm working the crowd, trying to get a few quotes for my

story. But people are trying to pry into the particulars of my past and I am ticked.

"Why would anybody in their right mind" give up the chance of an operatic career "for this?" says some other woman, who points her long nose at my reporter's notebook.

The cynical journalist in me doubts that Klein really remembers me all that well. A day earlier when we talked, I told him I had graduated from Music and Art and that my name had been Jill Moreland. I think he called the school, asked them to check my records and talked to some of my former teachers who told him about me. I was a good example for his speech. And a few compliments to pump up the ego of a reporter covering him couldn't hurt.

"I hope I didn't embarrass you?" he says after the woman with the long nose departs.

"No," I say, and smile. I feel bad. When I feel this bad I want to slip into silk pajamas, eat chocolate brownies, drink champagne and watch Fred Astaire.

At home, after Klein's speech, I bite into a brownie and think: He might not have used me as a convenient anecdote if he knew how much I mourned the state of my gift.

My voice is now a lover that comes and goes. I am euphoric in its presence. And even when it fades—because of misuse at a young age, chronic throat problems since infancy, fatigue at an older age from the daily strain of being a reporter, and just age—I can induce the euphoria through memory. The exhilaration of a beautiful and powerful sound, self-created, produces a high . . . leaves one light-headed . . . touches the same pleasure center as sex and cocaine. . . . Recall is enough to induce the sensations.

And when that self-induced high generates a response—applause—it is the ultimate drug. I was never so adored, I believed, as when I sang. When I sang, even my father looked at me with love. When I sang, people who said I had "personality" saw me onstage and told me I was beautiful, too.

I don't sing anymore.

When I think I know why, I realize I am still not sure.

There is no Fred Astaire on TV. I am a low-tech person, so I don't own a VCR and can't rent him. So I put on Verdi. His was the first music I heard floating from the tower of the building that housed Music and Art.

The school was on Convent Avenue then, a few blocks north of our Harlem apartment, a few streets past the Church of the Annunciation, where my mother had tried in vain to have me baptized. I don't know how I'd missed the building before, with its Gothic spires and gargoyles. I had combed the neighborhood since moving there more than a year before, often venturing up Convent Avenue with my bag of barbecue potato chips and a dill pickle, the sound of Motown in my head. Perhaps there had been silence when I passed the building before. But as I approached it that day, my brain drenched with Stevie Wonder's "Fingertips," I heard thunderous music:

> *Dies irae, dies illa,*
> *solvet saeclum in favilla*
> *teste David cum Sibylla*
> *Quantus tremor est futurus,*
> *quando judex est venturus,*
> *cuncta stricte discussurus!*

> *Day of wrath and doom impending,*
> *David's word with Sibyl's blending:*
> *Heaven and earth in ashes ending.*
> *Oh, what fear man's bosom rendeth,*
> *When from heaven the judge descendeth,*
> *On whose sentence all dependeth!*

# Has-beens Who Never Were

I had never heard so powerful a chorus singing live before. I stood on the corner with my mouth open. Then they stopped . . . began again. . . . And I heard her . . . a disembodied soprano voice whose sound fell to my skin as silk would. *Requiem aeternam dona eis, Domine, et lux perpetua luceat eis.* ("Eternal rest grant unto them, O Lord, and let perpetual light shine upon them.") I would learn one day that I was hearing the end of Verdi's *Requiem.*

I walked home slowly. What was that place? I wondered. No one was home when I got there. I pulled out some 78 recordings that were stored in the cabinet of an old combination radio and phonograph that stood in our long apartment hallway. There was another, modern, phonograph in the living room—my father's part of the house—but I liked the relic better. It was broken. It had a short. But if you spun the turntable manually to get it going, it played well for a while. I put on the first Sarah Vaughan record I ever heard, "The Lord's Prayer." I think "Sometimes I Feel Like a Motherless Child" was on the flip side.

Nat King Cole and Louis Armstrong were among the 78s too. But I kept playing Sarah. Her voice had the same ethereal quality I'd heard floating from the Gothic tower.

That night, I lay in bed singing to myself. It must have been an Indian summer, or an unusual mid-September in New York, because school had just started but it was very hot. The air conditioner in my room was on. No one, I thought, could hear me above its rumble.

My mother knocked on my door and came in. "Sweetheart," she said; she was smiling, her voice was gentle. I could tell she didn't want to say the words. "Your father says it's late. You should be asleep. Please stop singing."

The next day I asked Mrs. Johnson, my fifth-grade music teacher, "What is that place? What do they do in there?" When she told me it was a special high school for the arts, I wanted to know how I could get in it. She told me I had to audition, and to "work on your vibrato." I had too much of it, she insisted. From that moment, I spent every day till I was fifteen preparing to enter Music and Art.

My first year in the school was fine. But the second year, I lost my voice. I am still not certain why it happened. But my voice was so weak, I couldn't pass the audition to enter New York's All City Chorus. The director, John Motley, could not understand it. Just months before, I'd been the soloist in a concert at Columbia University's McMillin Hall, singing music arranged by him. The piece was a German folk song demanding a lyric soprano with perfect control and a stratospheric vocal reach. The concert had been recorded, probably the only recording of me in perfect voice. Despite the rigors of that performance, I couldn't get through a simple song for the choral audition.

"What happened?" asked a girl I had gone to junior high school with. Hers was not a sympathetic inquiry. She had been my musical rival in school, always placing second to me.

"I don't know," I said. "I've been having vocal problems for months." My father had been back for months, too. My parents had separated, but my mother, always seeking Ozzie and Harriet heaven, let him move into our Flatbush brownstone. I never considered the connections between him and my failing vocal powers at the time. Perhaps there were none. But every now and then, when the fog lifts about those years, I glimpse the child and her father standing in a shaft of light surrounded by the dark: He is seated on the bed in his boxer shorts, awestruck and speaking tenderly after I have sung. "My girl, you have the celestial vibration." Then he stands and touches the top of my head with the flat of his palm. I am nine and cannot see his face because he is standing so close, and my head doesn't reach beyond his bare chest. But I do not need to see him. I feel what is welling inside him and walk away self-satisfied.

But then I am thirteen. My father walks to the front of the auditorium where I have just performed. I remember the song, "Summertime." The aisles are filled with the departing crowd. Both my father and mother are standing nearby. But in my mind, my daddy and I are again alone, standing in that single column of light. He is speaking to me, but seems as physically distant as it is possible to be and still talk without shouting. "Very good, indeed," he says, then reaches into his pocket and pulls out a ten-dollar bill. The infinite distance is only imagined and immediately I feel the cash pressed into my palm. That was the night of my first paying gig.

I had no pockets, I had no purse, and I clutched the ten until my hand felt numb. But I could feel, even at that age, how lonely my father must have been, unable to find a suitable expression of his love for me or anyone else.

The weight I ultimately attached to my ability to sing well— no, perform perfectly—is tied to the love and appreciation my father articulated only when he heard me sing.

Even in recent years, when I have resumed voice lessons, the fear of failing at something that once defined me so totally paralyzed my voice—either that or some virus would take hold of me and provide a clinical reason for my disabled sound.

In my early adolescence I made no connection between my psyche and my throat. I suffered from the usual case of nerves before a performance until I was sixteen. But after that, it was torture for me to control my stage fright.

One afternoon, while taping a concert for National Public Radio, I had an anxiety attack and lost control of my voice, even though I'd already sung two art songs perfectly. I had been chosen by Music and Art to represent the school in a special series of radio recitals. But I suddenly choked. I went on with the taping, but it was a lost cause. I sounded breathy and amateurish. I pleaded with the school to scrap the broadcast. They did.

I couldn't comprehend what was happening to me. But the voice hides nothing; the instrument and the artist are indivisible.

Anna Ext, one of the school's most venerated voice teachers (she was featured on *60 Minutes* once in a segment about her former star pupil, mezzo-soprano Julia Migenes), told me flatly one day, "You are emotionally unstable." She could have said "Your hair is brown" in the same tone. She didn't bother to ask what was going on in my life. She just left me to think I was crazy. Perhaps she didn't mean to be unkind. Perhaps she held the romantic notion that great talent and madness frequently cohabit. I certainly felt crazy back then. And she certainly felt I had a great instrument.

To affirm her confidence in my gift, if not my sanity, Madame Ext recommended I be placed in the school's solo voice class, Music and Art's singing elite. It bolstered my confidence.

Unlike the television and movie versions of the school, there was little dancing in the hallways and few sudden bursts into pop songs by members of the student body. Jazz and popular music were not forbidden in the school—great jazz artists were occasional guest performers. But our formal training was strictly in the European classical tradition. Students indulged in pop, rock, soul and jazz after school. In my early teens, I still had my sights set on the Metropolitan Opera's stage. (No, that's not quite true. The New York City Opera had endeared itself to me because I could afford their tickets, and I never missed a Saturday afternoon performance during the City Opera's season.) Nonetheless, I decided to take a break from the classical world.

I entered New York's 1969 equivalent of *Star Search*. It was called "New Groove '69," a talent show sponsored by M-G-M

Records and WNEW-TV. The show toured through New York City giving benefit performances in schools and hospitals, then culminated in a contest on the stage of the Brooklyn Academy of Music, judged by music industry executives, performers and disc jockeys.

I belted a torchy version of "You're Gonna Hear from Me," accompanied by a wonderful big band. I won. I got the title of M-G-M Records' "Best New Pop Vocalist of 1969." After the show, a man claiming to be a Motown representative asked me to audition for the label. I demurely told him I had plans to be an opera singer and wasn't interested. I don't think I blew anything. I remember the little-girl-would-you-like-some-candy look in his watery eyes.

Nonetheless, I was willing to take the winner's prize: an audition with the late Joe Raposo for the Skitch Henderson show.

Relying on my own counsel, I thought it wise to sing something drastically different from the showstopper I'd won with. I wanted to show my versatility, my vocal range. I sang "It Might as Well Be Spring." I sang it as unembellished as Rodgers and Hammerstein had written it.

Raposo, who had been one of the "New Groove '69" judges, told me my voice was beautiful. But my style was not commercial enough.

I rarely react to anything immediately. As with other setbacks, I absorbed that one and took it as a lesson. I had to find my own style.

One afternoon in solo voice class I decided to try out "You're Gonna Hear from Me." Mrs. Mandel, our teacher and head of the voice department at the time, didn't mind if we occasionally went outside of the classical repertoire. Many students in the school were already professionals, singing in Broadway shows. Mandel was as interested in our perfecting our skills as interpreters of songs—becoming actors—as she was in teaching us the basic repertoire.

I gave her the music to "You're Gonna Hear from Me." Like most of my classmates, she'd never heard me sing a popular song.

"Fascinating," she said when I finished. "Very good, the voice is quite different." She meant that the character of my voice was totally different when I used my lower register. I sounded like a different singer. I had nearly a five-octave range; I could make my voice do almost anything.

And my classmates, especially the black ones, looked at me with new respect. "I didn't think you could sing anything but that bel canto stuff," one girl teased.

It was all beautiful singing. But until very recently, anybody with a voice who chose to study music formally had to do so in the European classical tradition—this is the basis of good vocal technique for any singer. But performing anything outside of the classical repertoire was viewed with contempt by most of the musical establishment. There was no such thing as a jazz vocal music major at American schools when I was a student. But it was becoming clear to me, as I sat in our Flatbush living room—lights out at 2:00 A.M., sipping vodka on the sly, listening to Miles play "My Funny Valentine," Sarah sing "You Go to My Head," Bird blow "Embraceable You"—that I wanted to stand on a stage in a strapless blue gown and sing beside a man with a horn.

I loved the peer approval I received when I sang jazz, pop and gospel. I was more relaxed when I wasn't singing classical music, too. But it had been drummed into my head that if one was going to be an "artist," one had to perform within the realm of "high" culture.

All this added to my adolescent confusion. About this time, I started popping the Thorazine samples I found in the doctor's office I worked in after school. I was so drugged some days, I walked into the walls at Music and Art. I fell off the stage one day in solo voice class. My suicidal impulses increased, and I finally sought therapy.

After months in therapy, my acute depression subsided, my anxiety attacks abated and my simmering sexuality erupted. I spent the last year and a half of high school in mostly perfect voice. I ran for class president braless, sporting an Afro, wearing big, round dark glasses and a micro-mini dress and offering a platform based on nothing that interested my classmates. (I don't even remember what it was.) I lost.

No matter, I was on a roll. I decided to use the school's vast talent to entertain patients in hospitals. With the help of students who'd go on to be award-winning performers (like Ben Harney, a Tony winner for *Dreamgirls*), we organized the best show then running in New York.

People who'd mistaken my insecurity and depression for snobbery were suddenly friendly. Especially several male teachers, one of whom was fired for making sexual overtures to me.

At rehearsals for my high school graduation, it was announced that I'd won the school's vocal music award. I would have been devastated, I think, if I hadn't. But I was shocked when they called me to the stage to receive something called the Simon Simeon Award from the mayor's office for social service to the city of New York—just because I wanted to entertain sick people. How, as I became older, could I have forgotten that one needn't abandon art for social activism?

The day I graduated with my class at Carnegie Hall—dressed in an African gown—guess who helped lead the Black Power chant from the audience as a contingent of blacks walked across the stage with the African liberation flag? Richard Klein had been warned: Allow the red, black and green flag of the Black Liberation Movement onstage or we'll disrupt the ceremony.

From the balcony of Carnegie Hall, white parents were shouting, "Nazis, Nazis."

A black parent looked toward the balcony wearily and said, "Oh, shut up." Then looked at me just as disgustedly.

Ten rows directly behind me, I heard my mother gasp each time I punched the air with the Black Power salute. After the ceremony she grabbed me by the neck and lifted me out of Carnegie Hall. "That was very nice," she growled as she dragged me down the aisle.

After that, my mother reluctantly realized she'd have to steel herself in preparation for my full metamorphosis.

Two years after my high school graduation, I am rushing to my cousin Karen's wedding in a big Brooklyn Catholic church. It is a blustery day in late autumn. I am in full African regalia, with a wool coat over it, and I am wearing sandals in the snow.

"No," I tell my mother, my big toe a brighter red than my nose as we meet in the church vestibule. "I'm not cold." Hell no. I'm an African.

During the summers and holidays of my college years, I lived in Newark, the headquarters for the Congress of African People. Its chairman was the major literary figure of the Black Arts Movement of the sixties and seventies and a major force in the Pan-African political movement, Amiri Baraka.

The rest of the year, I was a student at Boston University. I decided in my senior year of high school that I did not want to go to a conservatory. I was tired of being around people whose sole preoccupation was music. I wanted to be as intellectually challenged as I was artistically. Boston University wasn't my first choice of schools. I wanted to go to Montreal and study at McGill University. But Canada was overrun with Americans during the Vietnam War era and the school refused to accept any more U.S. citizens.

BU seemed an acceptable alternative: it was close to New York but got me away from home; it was in a city I was familiar with from childhood stays with my aunt Rae and it had a good music department—but, it turned out, an extremely conservative one. I don't think anyone in that school uttered the name of a twentieth-century composer without fear.

The first day I walked into the building, however, a group of students were performing in what they considered the modern mode. A half dozen kids surrounded a black upright piano and sang the corniest interpretation of Broadway show tunes I'd ever heard.

My "It Might as Well Be Spring" days were over. After all, during my last year at Music and Art I'd studied theory with the great jazz flautist Yusef Lateef. And I'd spent most of my summer in Greenwich Village hanging out in jazz clubs. Within a year of entering college, I heard, at a birthday party for Baraka, the greatest pure jazz singer on the planet: Betty Carter. There was no turning back.

My sophomore year, I wrote a new curriculum for the school that, I thought, brought it into the twentieth century. Among other things, it called for a recognition of non-Western music and the establishment of a division of ethnomusicology.

When I completed my proposed curriculum, I demanded a meeting with the university's new president, John Silber—the tough, conservative Texan intent on ridding the campus of radical students and professors, as well as making the academically uneven school uniformly first-rate.

He received me cordially. He was surprised that a teenager had made so sound and thorough a proposal. He was never condescending. It was clear he respected intelligent people who presented their case rationally—even if he disagreed. At least that was his manner behind closed doors with a student, back then.

More recently, I have interviewed him for the *Los Angeles Times* on the issue of expanding the traditional Western civilization curriculum to include ethnic studies. He agreed that the classical literature of other cultures—Confucian philosophy, for example—should be studied in addition to the Western classics. But he generally ranted and raved like a rabid animal over the phone, spouting the right-wing intellectual line on the sanctity of a traditional Western education, and our Greek and Roman heritage, and so on.

No matter how attentive he was to my concerns when I was a student, he didn't go for the cultural pluralism line back then, either. My proposal had no impact on the music curriculum.

But the music school was having an impact on me, despite its conservatism. There, I found the best voice teacher I ever had, Ruth Thompson. I'd been studying voice privately while at Music and Art, but neither the group instruction I received at Music and Art nor my private teacher had taught me proper vocal technique.

Thompson made me start at the beginning, none of the big Verdi and Puccini arias I'd been singing. I learned again, but with proper technique, the Italian and German art songs I'd been taught at Music and Art. Then we moved on to Mozart.

I was a quick study. In master classes, older students and Thompson told me I had more than a fine instrument. I had the electricity found in great voices.

One afternoon, after my lesson, I turned to Thompson. It was the end of the first semester of my sophomore year. Her studio was always dimly lit, I remember, and the Boston sky was a dirty gray.

"I'm leaving," I told her. I'd been watching the formation of

# Has-beens Who Never Were

my mouth in the mirror for weeks as I practiced "Musetta's Waltz" from *La Bohème*. How was singing "Quando me'n vo" going to change the world, improve the lot of poor people and people of color across the planet? I had asked myself between Puccini's lyrics.

If I was going to sing, I told her, I was going to sing jazz. And since I couldn't study that at BU, I might as well get my degree in something more useful.

Thompson looked up from the piano keyboard. Her eyes were full of contempt. "You would give up the chance of an opera career to sing jazz, that junk that anybody off the street can do?"

If I had any doubts about my decision at that moment, her cultural chauvinism was precisely the provocation I needed to stand my ground.

I had decided to get my undergraduate degree in journalism. I didn't just want to write, though; I wanted to own a newspaper one day, or a radio or television station. I wanted to help revolutionize the way people viewed the world and their place in it. And though I'd always taken my writing skills for granted—it was just something that I could do—I was now enamored with the beauty and power of language. I'd read and heard Baraka. Talk about black magic poetry. This was music, too. And its message shot down all the cultural imperialists like my voice teacher. It took aim at the psyche of black people gagging on a diet of self-hate for generations, and preached the worth of our own aesthetic and intellectual values.

But while I was reaching some valid conclusions about the world, I was doing so without the tempering insight of life experience. (That may be as good a definition of youth as any.)

Arrogantly and ignorantly, I presumed myself the most rational assessor of the world around me. I knew what was best. And my will has always been such that no one seriously tried to dissuade me when I made my decision. I abandoned the blueprint I'd created for my life from the age of three. In doing so, I'd forgotten the intimate power of a song to change a heart. This was the era of the soapbox.

The message from the nationalist soapbox was collective self-esteem, but based on a cultural chauvinism that became indistinguishable from the racist mentality we claimed to be fighting. Self-love, self-respect predicated on hating other people—white people in general and the vicious scapegoating of Jews in particular—was the ultimate contradiction of the cultural nationalist movement. That contradiction—among many others—would compel me to leave CAP. But that was years away.

In the summer of 1971, Baraka named me Itabari, a Swahili corruption of the Arabic Itibari. It means an esteemed person or one in whom you can place your trust or faith. Several years later, my mother provided my last name, Njeri, which is Kikuyu and means "worthy of a warrior." (Sexist, Ma, but I get your drift. Later, she claimed the sentiment was sincere but she didn't know I'd really use the name.)

I spent my college years as a political organizer for CAP, probably the most sophisticated Pan-African nationalist organization of the era, due to Baraka's intellectual leadership, as well as that of his wife, Amina Baraka. But like most nationalist organizations, it was a bastion of sexism—women bowing and scraping before men. It was puritanical—no sex outside of marriage, which I think nobody but me followed. But I took everything literally in those days. I gave up my birth control pills when I entered the organization and halted a very active sex life begun at seventeen. (Remember those posters with different sexual positions for every astrological sign—you know, the one that glowed under a black light? Well, I met an Indian graduate student, who looked like Zubin Mehta in his prime, at an orgy my freshman year. We became great friends, mastering every pose on the poster and adding some new ones. This man was the walking Kamasutra. I was really committed to the revolution to give him up.)

Baraka, I realize now, was a father figure to me. I was a teenager when I met him and joined the organization, just beginning to assert my individuality. Suddenly, I had to suppress my personality to conform to the organization. It was a hard fit. At heart, I was a rebellious, angry child who'd repressed her feelings to survive in an alcoholic family. I was making a similar adaption while in CAP because I felt the organization was the key to revolutionizing black people's self-image and gaining political empowerment. And if I had to relinquish all my bourgeois tendencies—as I was told—to achieve that goal, I was ready to purge myself. There was a lot to purge. I was light-skinned, so it was assumed that I thought myself better than darker-skinned black people. My only religious background was Catholic—when they found that out they knew I was near hopeless. And I'd been singing the devil's unadulterated music—opera. No one in the organization liked my voice, except when they heard me sing jazz. But I did win some respect because I could act. I was a natural comic. Baraka put me in his plays. During rehearsals, I'd catch him falling out of his chair laughing at me. He'd look at me with the kind of delight I'd seen in my father's eyes when I sang.

But after three years in the organization, I decided to leave. It was stifling. Baraka, a cosmopolite and intellectual renegade, had seen firsthand the world I wanted to experience. Members of the organization—we all lived together but in various locations—were told that the world outside was racist and bourgeois. That's why we didn't need to read *The New York Times*. We should live vicariously, through Baraka.

Leaving the organization was like leaving the convent. I tried to do it in person, but didn't have the guts. Several months after my first attempt, I mailed back my uniform—my black orthopedic-styled shoes, my long black jacket, my long black skirt.

Though I'd left BU's School of Fine and Applied Arts for its School of Public Communications, I hadn't abandoned performing.

When I wasn't acting with Baraka's theater company, the Spirit House Movers, I was performing with a group called Blakluv in Boston. We did a lot of university concerts, prison gigs, local TV and radio concerts throughout New England.

At the same time, I'd gotten my first paying job as a journalist while still in school. I was a reporter for National Public Radio in Boston, then a producer and host of my own syndicated show, "The Pan-African News Report," as well as a reporter and co-producer for several other news programs.

I was carrying a double load at school, too, because I had switched majors and needed additional credits to graduate on time. Despite my schedule, I was an A student and a University Trustee Scholar.

I had a lot of energy.

I was doing a lot of sublimating.

Several months after I finished college, I collapsed from exhaustion.

I was out of a job, too. WBUR-FM, the NPR station for which I worked, had its budget cut. Last hired, first canned.

I spent the rest of the year singing part-time, doing secretarial work part-time and deprogramming myself from the CAP experience. The latter meant that I could show my legs and cleavage again. But I couldn't expect everybody to speak to me in Swahili when we met. Nor could I expect everybody to share the same code of conduct, as we did in CAP: cooperative effort for a shared goal, trustworthiness, honesty and a genuine love and understanding of black people and culture.

# Has-beens Who Never Were

My major post-CAP cultural experience came when I toured with Mr. "Love Won't Let Me Wait" in the land of the doo-wops. That, of course, contributed to my decision to go to graduate school and write instead of sing for my living.

I do not know if I made the right decision. I do find a balance as a writer I never had as a musician—perhaps because I meant the singing to serve me in ways it could not. It was an escape. It was an act of self-healing. Richard Klein might have trod more gently had he known that.

But singing never satisfied me intellectually. Writing feeds both my creative and intellectual cravings. And there is some solace in thinking that, if I'm good enough, what I create as a writer could last forever. I look on the shelf where two copies of my father's book, *The Tolono Station and Beyond*, sit side by side. It is palpable evidence that he created something of value in the world. A song is such an ephemeral thing.

Yet, beside my father's book is one he gave me when I graduated from Music and Art, Gustav Kobbe's *Complete Opera Book*. Inside it he wrote: "To Jill the Pill—A song is but a little thing, but what a joy it is to sing."

The decade was about to end when I started my first newspaper job. The seventies might have been the disco generation for some, but it was a continuation of the Black Power, post–Civil Rights era for me. Of course in some parts of America it was still the pre–Civil Rights era. And that was the part of America I wanted to explore. As a good reporter I needed a sense of the whole country, not just the provincial Northeast Corridor in which I was raised.

I headed for Greenville ("Pearl of the Piedmont"), South Carolina.

"*Wheeere,*" some people snarled, their nostrils twitching, their mouths twisted so their top lips went slightly to the right, the bottom ones way down and to the left, "did you get *that* name from?"

Itabiddy. Etabeedy. Etabeeree. Eat a berry. Mata Hari. Theda Bara. And one secretary in the office of the Greenville Urban League told her employer: "It's Ms. Idi Amin."

Then, and now, there are a whole bunch of people who greet me with: "Hi, Ita." They think "Bari" is my last name. Even when they don't, they still want to call me "Ita." When I tell them my first name is Itabari, they say, "Well, what do people call you for short?"

"They don't call me anything for short," I say. "The name is Itabari."

Sophisticated white people, upon hearing my name, approach me as would a cultural anthropologist finding a piece of exotica right in his own living room. This happens a lot, still, at cocktail parties.

"Oh, what an unusual and beautiful name. Where are you from?"

"Brooklyn," I say. I can see the disappointment in their eyes. Just another homegrown Negro.

Then there are other white people who, having heard my decidedly northeastern accent, will simply say, "What a lovely name," and smile knowingly, indicating that they saw *Roots* and understand.

Then there are others, black and white, who for different reasons take me through this number:

"What's your *real* name?"

"Itabari Njeri is my real, legal name," I explain.

"Okay, what's your *original* name?" they ask, often with eyes rolling, exasperation in their voices.

After Malcolm X, Muhammad Ali, Kareem Abdul-Jabaar, Ntozake Shange and Kunta Kinte, who, I ask, should be exasperated by this question-and-answer game?

# Has-beens Who Never Were

Nevertheless, I explain, "Because of slavery, black people in the Western world don't usually know their original names. What you really want to know is what my slave name was."

Now this is where things get tense. Four hundred years of bitter history, culture and politics between blacks and whites in America is evoked by this one term, "slave name."

Some white people wince when they hear the phrase, pained and embarrassed by this reminder of their ancestors' inhumanity. Further, they quickly scrutinize me and conclude that mine was a post–Emancipation Proclamation birth. "You were never a slave."

I used to be reluctant to tell people my slave name unless I surmised that they wouldn't impose their cultural values on me and refuse to use my African name. I don't care anymore. When I changed my name, I changed my life, and I've been Itabari for more years now than I was Jill. Nonetheless, people will say: "Well, that's your *real* name, you were born in America and that's what I am going to call you." My mother tried a variation of this on me when I legalized my traditional African name. I respectfully made it clear to her that I would not tolerate it. Her behavior, and subsequently her attitude, changed.

But many black folks remain just as skeptical of my name as my mother was.

"You're one of those black people who changed their name, huh," they are likely to begin. "Well, I still got the old slave master's Irish name," said one man named O'Hare at a party. This man's defensive tone was a reaction to what I call the "blacker than thou" syndrome perpetrated by many black nationalists in the sixties and seventies. Those who reclaimed their African names made blacks who didn't do the same thing feel like Uncle Toms.

These so-called Uncle Toms couldn't figure out why they should use an African name when they didn't know a thing about Africa. Besides, many of them were proud of their names, no matter how they had come by them. And it should be noted that after the Emancipation Proclamation in 1863, four million black people changed their names, adopting surnames such as Freeman, Freedman and Liberty. They eagerly gave up names that slave masters had imposed upon them as a way of identifying their human chattel.

Besides names that indicated their newly won freedom, blacks chose common English names such as Jones, Scott and Johnson. English was their language, America was their home, and they wanted names that would allow them to assimilate as easily as possible.

Of course, many of our European surnames belong to us by birthright. We are the legal as well as "illegitimate" heirs to the names Jefferson, Franklin, Washington, et al; and in my own family, Lord.

Still, I consider most of these names to be by-products of slavery, if not actual slave names. Had we not been enslaved, we would not have been cut off from our culture, lost our indigenous languages and been compelled to use European names.

The loss of our African culture is a tragic fact of history, and the conflict it poses is a profound one that has divided blacks many times since Emancipation: Do we accept the loss and assimilate totally or do we try to reclaim our culture and synthesize it with our present reality?

A new generation of black people in America is reexamining the issues raised by the cultural nationalists and Pan-Africanists of the sixties and seventies: What are the cultural images that appropriately convey the "new" black aesthetic in literature and art?

The young Afro-American novelist Trey Ellis has asserted

that the "New Black Aesthetic shamelessly borrows and reassembles across both race and class lines." It is not afraid to embrace the full implications of our hundreds of years in the New World. We are a new people who need not be tied to externally imposed or self-inflicted cultural parochialism. Had I understood that as a teenager, I might still be singing today.

Even the fundamental issue of identity and nomenclature, raised by Baraka and others twenty years ago, is back on the agenda: Are we to call ourselves blacks or African-Americans?

In reality, it's an old debate. "Only with the founding of the American Colonization Society in 1816 did blacks recoil from using the term African in referring to themselves and their institutions," the noted historian and author Sterling Stuckey pointed out in an interview with me. They feared that using the term "African" would fuel white efforts to send them back to Africa. But they felt no white person had the right to send them back when they had slaved to build America.

Many black institutions retained their African identification, most notably the African Methodist Episcopal Church. Changes in black self-identification in America have come in cycles, usually reflecting the larger dynamics of domestic and international politics.

The period after World War II, said Stuckey, "culminating in the Cold War years of Roy Wilkins's leadership of the NAACP," was a time of "frenzied integrationism." And there was "no respectable black leader on the scene evincing any sort of interest in Africa—neither the NAACP or the Urban League."

This, he said, "was an example of historical discontinuity, the likes of which we, as a people, had not seen before." Prior to that, for more than a century and a half, black leaders were Pan-Africanists, including Frederick Douglass. "He recognized," said Stuckey, "that Africa was important and that somehow one had to redeem the motherland in order to be genuinely respected in the New World."

The Reverend Jesse Jackson has, of course, placed on the national agenda the importance of blacks in America restoring their cultural, historical and political links with Africa.

But what does it really mean to be called an African-American?

"Black" can be viewed as a more encompassing term, referring to all people of African descent. "Afro-American" and "African-American" refer to a specific ethnic group. I use the terms interchangeably, depending on the context and the point I want to emphasize.

But I wonder: As the twenty-first century breathes down our necks—prodding us to wake up to the expanding mélange of ethnic groups immigrating in record numbers to the United States, inevitably intermarrying, and to realize the eventual reshaping of the nation's political imperatives in a newly multicultural society—will the term "African-American" be as much of a racial and cultural obfuscation as the term "black"? In other words, will we be the only people, in a society moving toward cultural pluralism, viewed to have no history and no culture? Will we just be a color with a new name: African-American?

Or will the term be—as I think it should—an ethnic label describing people with a shared culture who descended from Africans, were transformed in (as well as transformed) America and are genetically intertwined with myriad other groups in the United States?

Such a definition reflects the historical reality and distances us from the fallacious, unscientific concept of separate races when there is only one: *Homo sapiens.*

But to comprehend what should be an obvious definition requires knowledge and a willingness to accept history.

# Has-beens Who Never Were

When James Baldwin wrote *Nobody Knows My Name*, the title was a metaphor—at the deepest level of the collective African-American psyche—for the blighting of black history and culture before the nadir of slavery and since.

The eradication or distortion of our place in world history and culture is most obvious in the popular media. Liz Taylor—and, for an earlier generation, Claudette Colbert—still represent what Cleopatra—a woman of color in a multiethnic society, dominated at various times by blacks—looks like.

And in American homes, thanks to reruns and cable, a new generation of black kids grow up believing that a simpleton shouting "Dy-no-mite!" is a genuine reflection of Afro-American culture, rather than a white Hollywood writer's stereotype.

More recently, *Coming to America*, starring Eddie Murphy as an African prince seeking a bride in the United States, depicted traditional African dancers in what amounted to a Las Vegas stage show, totally distorting the nature and beauty of real African dance. But with every burlesque-style pelvic thrust on the screen, I saw blacks in the audience burst into applause. They think that's African culture, too.

And what do Africans know of us, since blacks don't control the organs of communication that disseminate information about us?

"No!" screamed the mother of a Kenyan man when he announced his engagement to an African-American woman who was a friend of mine. The mother said marry a European, marry a white American. But please, not one of those low-down, ignorant, drug-dealing, murderous black people she had seen in American movies. Ultimately, the mother prevailed.

In Tanzania, the travel agent looked at me indignantly. "Njeri, that's Kikuyu. What are you doing with an African name?" he demanded.

I'd been in Dar es Salaam about a month and had learned that Africans assess in a glance the ethnic origins of the people they meet.

Without a greeting, strangers on the street in Tanzania's capital would comment, "Oh, you're an Afro-American or West Indian."

"Both."

"I knew it," they'd respond, sometimes politely, sometimes not.

Or, people I got to know while in Africa would mention, "I know another half-caste like you." Then they would call in the "mixed-race" person and say, "Please meet Itabari Njeri." The darker-complected African, presumably of unmixed ancestry, would then smile and stare at us like we were animals in the zoo.

Of course, this "half-caste" (which I suppose is a term preferable to "mulatto," which I hate, and which every person who understands its derogatory meaning—"mule"—should never use) was usually the product of a mixed marriage, not generations of ethnic intermingling. And it was clear from most "half-castes" I met that they did not like being compared to so mongrelized and stigmatized a group as Afro-Americans.

I had minored in African studies in college, worked for years with Africans in the United States and had no romantic illusions as to how I would be received in the motherland. I wasn't going back to find my roots. The only thing that shocked me in Tanzania was being called, with great disdain, a "white woman" by an African waiter. Even if the rest of the world didn't follow the practice, I then assumed everyone understood that any known or perceptible degree of African ancestry made one "black" in America by law and social custom.

But I was pleasantly surprised by the telephone call I received two minutes after I walked into my Dar es Salaam hotel room.

# Has-beens Who Never Were

It was the hotel operator. "Sister, welcome to Tanzania. . . . Please tell everyone in Harlem hello for us." The year was 1978, and people in Tanzania were wearing half-foot-high platform shoes and dancing to James Brown wherever I went.

Shortly before I left, I stood on a hill surrounded by a field of endless flowers in Arusha, near the border of Tanzania and Kenya. A toothless woman with a wide smile, a staff in her hand and two young girls at her side, came toward me on a winding path. I spoke to her in fractured Swahili and she to me in broken English.

"I know you," she said smiling. "Wa-Negro." "Wa" is a prefix in Bantu languages meaning people. "You are from the lost tribe," she told me. "Welcome," she said, touching me, then walked down a hill that lay in the shadow of Mount Kilimanjaro.

I never told her my name, but when I told other Africans, they'd say: "*Emmmm*, Itabari. Too long. How about I just call you Ita."

# Coda

. . . the night he appeared by special invitation, he stood at my door without a hat. He looked different. He looked better than before. And as my mother pointed out, he hadn't looked bad in a hat. He was a rock-age Cary Grant dressed in leather, with a silver earring in his left lobe and dark curly hair with a lock in a pigtail at his nape.

He was gallant and daring, a mestizo Zorro who rode a motorcycle sometimes and drove a red Volvo other times. But I didn't know those particulars when we first met. Then, he was just a stranger, in a hat.

The hat was appropriate. I'd told my guests to break out their baddest berets, their sharpest chapeaus, their coolest kofias. Vivien Dacre Lord Reynolds—the most stylish mom to ever break down a brim—was coming to town. In her honor, I was turning my Los Angeles apartment into the Mad Hatter's salon. She needed a party. So did I.

A month before the bash my mother had called. "Maybe now your aunt will go into the hospital." It was the day after Aunt Rae's husband, Willie, had died. Aunt Rae, my mother theorized, could no longer use him—"I can't go anywhere. I can't leave Willie by himself"—as an excuse. I stood washing the dishes the day after Christmas listening to my mother's hopeful speculation. I decided not to tell her the obvious. A woman who stays in an apartment all Christmas Day with a dead man, eats a holiday dinner delivered by relatives, then, between mouthfuls, calmly says, "Yes, I know," when they discover the cold corpse in an armchair isn't going to rush for the nearest alcohol treatment center under her own steam. And she didn't.

So nurse Lord packed her bags and flew from her Florida home to New York, where she battled hospital bureaucracies, Aunt Rae's dementia and other assorted dysfunctional relatives.

In the midst of all that, Ma had to deal with Ruby—spitting mad again, after a period of relative calm, that she was imprisoned in a nursing home.

Until recent visits, my grandmother could be found seated in a straight chair beside her bed sorting the contents of her big black handbag—a file for all her important papers. She'd take out a wad of frayed, white, letter-size envelopes, bound with a rubber band, and inspect their contents. She'd do it for hours, muttering to herself their significance and the business she'd have to attend to when she got out of the home. She seldom got out of the home now. She was bedridden most of the time, crippled with arthritis.

But on a good day, she'd sit up for a few hours in her chair. It was a good day when Ma called in the midst of her mission to save Aunt Rae.

"And where," Grandma demanded of my mother, "is the two hundred dollars I told you to bring me? I told you to talk to Mama, I told you to talk to the lawyer, and to bring me my two hundred dollars."

"Mama" was my grandmother's mother—Alice Dacre Duncombe—dead for at least fifty years. And "the lawyer" was the man in cahoots with Aunt May, my grandmother's half sister, whom she accused of stealing her inheritance—her money, her property, her jewels in Jamaica. The material things that would

# Coda

have given her the status she lacked and craved so desperately. "Mama, what money are you talking about?" my mother asked. "There is no money, Mama."

"Whaaaaat!" Ruby said incredulously. "You mean . . . I'm a pauper?"

My mother laughed gently. "Yes, Mama, we're all paupers."

But the family had enough collective wealth, which my mother drew upon, to pay the back rent on Aunt Rae's co-op. Then Supernurse got my aunt hospitalized. Afterwards, she took her cousin Thelma—one of the few functional family members from my mother's generation—back to Aunt Rae's apartment to clean it out. They found the inevitable bottles of liquor hidden throughout the house. "I was tempted to take a few sips," my mother joked wearily. Later that day, when she called me from Brooklyn to tell me the status of her rescue mission, she admitted: "Your brother's out, the house is quiet and I've opened the bottle of May wine."

She'd put Aunt Rae in a month-long alcohol detoxification program. "But what are you going to do with her after that?" I asked pointedly.

"Just wait a minute now," she snapped defensively. "One thing at a time." I decided to drop it. My mother still would not or could not understand that alcoholism was an insidious disease that required more than the equivalent of a shot of penicillin. Given that, she was doing the best she could.

I heard nothing from Kay-Kay about Aunt Rae. She was emotionally paralyzed when it came to her mother. And her own life was in chaos. She'd left her lesbian Significant Other and moved in with a platonic friend, who was also gay. They'd both met a woman at the same time. The woman fell for my cousin and my cousin's new roommate became jealous. She demanded my cousin leave—just before Kay-Kay was to come visit me, about a month before the Mad Hatter's gala. Though

I feared my cousin's visit would turn into a week of neurotic gloom-and-doom happenings, she sounded emotionally strong on the phone and said she was coping with the chaos.

When she arrived in L.A. I rushed to the airport to meet her. "How are you?" I boomed as I hugged her.

"Get me to the nearest ACOA support group meeting *immediately*," she said through clenched teeth.

Right. So much for a fun-filled week in L.A. and San Francisco. After an eighty-hour workweek at the paper, with one more story to write before we left for San Francisco the next afternoon, I tracked down the nearest Adult Children of Alcoholics support group. It was cold and it was wet in L.A. as I shuttled between the office, home and the ACOA meeting in Hollywood (the leader was "a jerk," my cousin complained). It was colder and wetter in San Francisco. By the end of the week, I had my worst cold in twenty years. By the time my mother and fifty guests arrived for the Mad Hatter's fete a month later, I had tracheal bronchitis.

The evening of the party my phone rang: "This is Nicholas." I'd sent him, along with family members, a copy of the manuscript of my book for comment.

"I didn't know you were so bitter," he said. He also hadn't known, I learned from mutual friends, that indeed I was the tire slasher in the night. "I'm afraid to say anything to you. It may end up as a new chapter in the book."

I told him I couldn't talk to him then, I was preparing for a party. But we could speak the following week.

I was too tired and sick to really enjoy my own party, but few could tell. I had on a hat.

"And what do you do?" asked a guest who met me in an unlikely first encounter. I was cutting crudités in my black dress and wide-brimmed black hat. I didn't know the man; he had come with two acquaintances. And who the hell was he to ask

# Coda

what I did in that "what's your claim to fame" tone in my own house?

"Oh, this and that," I responded evenly.

"What does that mean?" he wanted to know.

"I write . . . I sing . . ."

"Can I help you with anything?" he wanted to know.

"You can mix those herbs with the sour cream," I directed.

"How much?" He fumbled with the sour cream. "Which ones?" He picked up the wrong bottle of herbs. "I'm not sure I know what to do here."

"Don't offer if you can't follow through," I said with a smile, then abandoned him.

I was too busy the rest of the evening to pay much attention to him. But as the party wound down and the guitarist I'd engaged for the evening played jazz softly in the living room, my bold guest sat beside me on the wood floor.

"This is a wonderful party," he told me. "Would you like a pillow?" he offered.

"No thank you," I told him, and continued talking to another guest beside me. When I rose, he took my hand to help me off the floor.

*Booommmmm!* Thunder. Lightning. He touched me. Time stopped. Nobody else was there, etc. But I was too busy playing host to deal with it then. Besides, he had come with somebody else and I don't play that stuff.

The next day: "Who was that handsome man?" my mother wanted to know.

"Oh, he came with an acquaintance. I don't really know him."

"He was really quite attractive, quite charming," she went on.

"Yeah," I said, "and quite arrogant." Pause. "And I like it."

My mother laughed.

He called.

"Yes," I said, "I found you attractive too." But what about the woman he came with? A friend, he said. A friend, she'd confirmed earlier.

I told him I was too busy to see him for several weeks. I was working on a magazine story that would occupy most of my days and nights for a while. But a day or two later, as I was rushing out the door to an interview, I remembered a going-away party for a friend.

"Ma"—my mother was still visiting me—"I'm in a hurry. Would you play social secretary for me?" I asked her to call him, invite him to the party and tell him I would call him back to confirm. She did. He said he was busy but would cancel his plans to be with me.

The night he came by special invitation, he threw jewelry and gardenias at my feet, then swept me off them.

He told me his mother was a Panamanian, his father a Hispanic, a former colonel in the U.S. army. Between them they'd produced this Latin lover with an Old World sense of honor and gallantry befitting an officer's son. But he is a child of the sixties, too; slightly rebellious and socially conscious in a hippie kind of way—Peace, Love, Save the Planet. And, at forty-one, he has learned some lessons from one bad marriage and happily wakes me in the morning with: "Honey, your breakfast is ready."

When I leave for work, he gets seriously miffed if I don't give him one last kiss, one more smile, one last look.

"What are we, Ozzie and Harriet?" I asked him. "I kissed you this morning. If I don't throw you a kiss from the car or glance up one more time, it's not that I don't care. I have work on my mind. Don't you?"

My electrical engineer with the stud in his ear looked at me with steady eyes. "You don't know what could happen to either

# Coda

of us. We might never see each other again. I hate it when you don't give me that last look."

I didn't dare laugh, he was so earnest. But when one is accustomed to the emotional equivalent of a man's foot pushing one out the door, rather than his pleas for "one last look," it takes some adjustment.

"See," he half teased, "you women claim you want commitment but when you get it you don't know how to act."

He answered the phone when Nicholas called again.

"Are you living with somebody?" Nick wanted to know.

"No," I told him, then listened to his complaints about the book. We agreed to disagree and said good-bye. But with this man, as Ruby would say, I knew every good-bye didn't mean gone.

I'm going to see Ruby in a few weeks. She is ninety-two now and has been asking for me constantly. I, of course, possess the handwritten version of her well-known funeral instructions: "Four flower cars. . . . And no, absolutely no in-laws in the first car. . . ." I think that last piece was meant for Willie, whom she didn't like. But he's dead now. I'll have to ask her if that instruction still holds.

While I held nothing against Willie, his sister is family enemy number one at the moment. She, a virtual stranger to us, took Aunt Rae out of the hospital without authorization.

"How could you allow such a thing?" I yelled over the phone in L.A. to the hospital social worker in New York.

"A-a-a-a," she stuttered nervously. "A-a-a family member authorized it. I called"—she paused to look through her case file—"an Alex Lord, your aunt's brother, and a Mrs. Vivien Lord Reynolds, her sister, and they agreed that she should be released."

I knew that was a lie and told her so.

"I did talk to them."

"You talked to them after the fact," I screamed.

"Well, there was no medical reason to keep your aunt. But she's still on the waiting list for a nursing home," the social worker assured me.

"She's an alcoholic," I shouted. "If you know anything about her case you know that she is unable to care for herself, she's lost the last eight years of her memory and she needs to be in a treatment program. What kind of incompetent are you?"

"Well, well, the family is so big—I never saw so many relatives with one patient—I didn't know who was who anymore," she argued lamely. "One day there were five cousins, sisters, sister-in-laws, a brother. We just assumed that the person who signed her out was an authorized family member."

My mother's voice was flat. "I'm dumbfounded. After all that work to get her in the hospital. It just never occurred to me that some stranger could walk in and take her out."

Aunt Glo wasn't upset though. "Your mother and Uncle Alex think people should just be thrown in nursing homes. That's what they did to your grandmother. But your aunt's too young. She should be left to live on her own if she wants."

I wouldn't be surprised if Aunt Glo had a hand in getting Willie's sister to take Aunt Rae out of the hospital. Though Aunt Rae might have orchestrated it herself, for all I know. Her diminished capacity hadn't affected her ability to scam. My mother says she found a way to get liquor while in the hospital, which isn't hard to believe. There are so many people in the city desperate for even chump change, all my aunt had to do was lay a dollar in somebody's palm.

Aunt Rae is supposed to move back to her own apartment and try to make it on her own. I don't think I'll visit her when I go to see Grandma next month. Ruby may be all my nerves can take. I know the first question out of her mouth will be "Did you get that bracelet appraised?"

# Coda

I've told her I don't need it appraised. I already know its real value. The bracelet is an inch wide, made of solid gold hammered into a band. On the clasp are paper-thin gold leaves studded with pearls. It was made in Panama about one hundred years ago and belonged to my great-grandmother Alice. The bracelet and some solid silver spoons are the only material evidence I have of Ruby's rich past. But they will not be my only connection with her when she's gone, I'm sure.

"When I'm dead," she once told Kay-Kay, "I will come to you. I will speak to you . . . warn you . . . protect you. But you must never answer any question I may ask. If you do, you'll be drawn to the other side with me, brought to an untimely death."

"She must have meant that for me too," I told my engineer.

"Is that what 'Every shut eye ain't sleep; every good-bye ain't gone' means?" he asked.

"It can mean that. It can mean lots of things."

"It sounds like a mighty Catholic concept to me, something the nuns used to tell us: 'God sees the evil you do.' "

"It means lots of things," I repeated, annoyed that he did not immediately grasp what to me was the obvious. "It's an endless spiritual connection," I said with exasperation. "A night with eyes . . . a—"

"Shhhhh. . . . Okay, I see. I hear you."

I am intolerant of him at times. While he is a romantic soul, I have discovered that, indeed, he has the mind of an engineer—too literal and pragmatic at times when intuitive understanding of my culture, my worldview is crucial to me.

We do not share the same cultural past. He is a Latin with no Latin culture, raised in a military and family environment that stressed Anglo conformity. He never lived in one place more than three years, and wherever he lived he was a loner. He can teach me about Frida Kahlo, of whom I was ignorant

243

till he introduced me to her work, and whitewater rafting—about which I'd prefer to remain ignorant.

But of foreign and domestic issues of culture and race so important to me, I tell him he has too little insight. Because he is mestizo, because he has so many friends who are Asian and black, it took a few weeks of my knowing him to fully comprehend the truth of what he told me early on: "I've been raised as a white, Anglo-Saxon Catholic." Then, one weekend in the woods, he mentioned he hadn't known what a minstrel show was till he saw a television documentary on the subject a few years ago. Yet he wanted to debate (he always wants to debate—I call him Dr. Whiz 'cause he thinks he knows it all) whether the minstrel show was a racist distortion of black culture or, as he seemed to think, imitation based on admiration of black culture by whites.

"Where did you go to school? What America did you grow up in?" I shrieked with my usual tact.

The minstrel show episode almost ended the relationship. But as I've come to know him, I realize that living, as he did, on military bases abroad, as well as in the United States, is not always the broadening experience some would assume. It seems to have thrust him into shifting states of isolation. And a childhood accident when he was about three—a fall into a lime pit that left his arms severely scarred, requiring years of plastic surgery—kept him in his own world throughout his childhood; a world of long walks in the woods and books filled with physics and astronomy.

"You have to talk to me like I'm a foreigner sometimes," he once said with hurt eyes after I'd attacked him for some perceived culturally insensitive comment. And then he took me into the mountains and showed me the outline of the Pleiades against the night sky.

"I'm open to learning about the things you care about. I'm

# Coda

intuitive about the things that count," he insisted as we sat within earshot of the roaring Pacific one bright day. "After all, Itabari, what is really important?" he asked, but did not wait for me to answer. "*We* are important," he said, dismissing all else, rocking me in his arms and teaching me to spend the day in lazy kisses . . .

# PERMISSION ACKNOWLEDGMENTS